D1255525

THE ARGYLLS IN KOREA

Frontispiece   ' Dinner pipes ' at Uibongju

THE ARGYLLS IN KOREA

Lieutenant-Colonel G. I. Malcolm
of Poltalloch

THOMAS NELSON AND SONS LIMITED

LONDON EDINBURGH PARIS MELBOURNE
TORONTO AND NEW YORK

THOMAS NELSON AND SONS LTD
Parkside Works Edinburgh 9
3 Henrietta Street London WC2
312 Flinders Street Melbourne C1
5 Parker's Buildings Burg Street Cape Town

THOMAS NELSON AND SONS (CANADA) LTD
91–93 Wellington Street West   Toronto 1

THOMAS NELSON AND SONS
19 East 47th Street New York 17

SOCIÉTÉ FRANÇAISE D'EDITIONS NELSON
25 rue Henri Barbusse Paris V⁰

———

First published September 1952

FOREWORD

IN writing the Foreword of this book I would like to say how cleverly the author has conveyed the extraordinary spirit of comradeship that existed amongst all ranks of the 27th Infantry Brigade, later known as the 27th Commonwealth Brigade, throughout their time in Korea.

In spite of living under very often appalling conditions, with none of the facilities of normal life, this great spirit was apparent always. I never quite understood this, but it was a considerable source of strength and inspiration to me, their commander. I think everyone was very much aware that we were the representatives of the British Commonwealth, and as such we had a great pride. Without exception, American supporting arms always liked being with us, and the cheerfulness of our soldiers was a source of amazement to them.

The author has mentioned volunteers from other battalions in Hong Kong—they came from the K.O.S.B., Royal Leicesters, and, to my amazement, one day I found that the second-in-command's driver was from my regiment, the Wiltshire Regiment, as remote from Scotland as almost anywhere. He was very happy and reckoned he was now as good a Jock as any. All these men had settled in and were content, which I think is a great tribute to Neilson and his officers.

After the fight at 282 and during the advance to the River Yalu, I always regarded the Argylls as my lucky battalion, for when I put them in the lead they seldom seemed to meet much opposition, whereas the Australians invariably did.

This account of the Argylls in Korea is a modest one, and perhaps readers who did not know this battalion might think that the enemy was not much in evidence and that there were only the hardships of the climate to contend with. That of course was far from being the case. For example, the account of the ' Cavalry Canter ' :

This operation was bad planning by American staff

officers who were out of touch with the battle, and was one of the few occasions when I failed to persuade my superiors to implement a sounder plan, which was for the Argylls to withdraw by the route which they eventually took. I then tried to open up their planned withdrawal route with the Australians but failed, as they ran into strong opposition. We had no contact with the Argylls at Brigade Headquarters and the night was an anxious one for all of us, as there appeared to be a good chance of the Argylls and Colonel Billy Harris's force being cut off. Leslie Neilson knew nothing of this until I told him after the event, and it is typical of him only to recount the facts as they appeared to him at the time, that no enemy were encountered.

Finally, no commander could have been better served than I was by all the officers and men of the 27th British Commonwealth Brigade, a good augury for the future as we were the first force to serve under United Nations Command.

The *esprit de corps* that we had in Korea is well expressed by Jimmy Stewart, my Argyll Brigade Major, who took over when Douglas Reith was killed, in a letter to me after he had returned to Hong Kong :

' About this time of year my thoughts dwell on those deep Wadis north of Yoju, and that unexplainable happiness which exists even amid beastliness—when passes are taken and catches held.'

B. A. COAD
Major-General

B.A.O.R., *May* 1952

PREFACE

This is neither a history nor a textbook. There is no moral to be drawn from it ; no tactical lessons to be learned. It is simply a tribute to a regular battalion doing, in unusual circumstances, the job for which it had been trained. I do not claim (nor do they) that officers and men did more than their duty. But I hope that my story will show that they acquitted themselves in the way that has been expected of all battalions of The Argyll and Sutherland Highlanders since the Regiment was raised.

As will be seen from the text my acknowledgments must be manifold, for I have been more editor than author. They are due principally to Lieutenant-General Sir Gordon Macmillan of Macmillan and Knap, who has not only made available to me all the material sent to the publishers at his instance, but also the personal correspondence which he himself received from the front.

Next I wish to acknowledge gratefully the help I have had from Colonel Neilson and Major Wilson who have read the MS and made valuable corrections to it. I also want to thank all officers and men of the Battalion and their relatives who have allowed me to make use of private letters and pictures.

Finally, my thanks are due to the historical section of the War Office for giving me access to official documents ; and to my wife, who drew the sketch for the diagram on page 41—I never could draw !

G. I. M.

Poltalloch 1952

vii

MAP TO ILLUSTRATE THE OPERATIONS OF THE ARGYLLS IN KOREA

MANCHURIA

Yalu River

NORTH KOREA

SEA OF JAPAN

Taech'ŏn
Pakch'ŏn
(Kunmori)
(Kunu-ri)
Sunch'ŏn
Ŭnsan
Sinanju
Yongyu
Sinjang
Ch'ŏngju
PYŎNGYANG
Yul-li
Chinnampo
HŬNGNAM

N

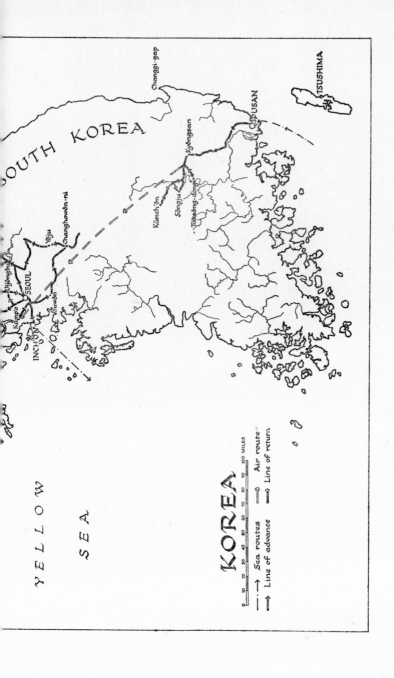

YELLOW

SEA

SOUTH KOREA

Changgi-gap

TSUSHIMA

Kyŏngsan

PUSAN

Kŭmch'ŏn

Sŏngju-dong

Tŭksŏng-dong

Chinju

Kŭmp'o

Uijŏngbu

SEOUL

Changhowŏn-ni

Suwŏn

INCH'ON

KOREA

```
0   10  20  30  40  50  60  70  80  90  100 MILES
```

····▶ Sea routes   ══▷ Air route
⟶ Line of advance   ═══▷ Line of return

CONTENTS

LIST OF PLATES

LIST OF PLATES

CHAPTER I

VOYAGE TO BATTLE

STARTING off for a war is much the same as starting off for any other purpose in the Army. However many orders and instructions and march tables and maps may have been issued, a battalion's first collective movement begins when a loud voice shouts : ' Outside with your rifles.' Nothing can really happen until this time-honoured and authentic order is given. As far as the 1st Battalion Argyll and Sutherland Highlanders was concerned, the Korean War proved no exception to this hallowed rule, and on Friday, 25th August 1950, these familiar lines could be heard all over their camp in the new territories of Hong Kong. They were greeted in the usual way that Jocks greet such things, but they occasioned no surprise. For they were only the executive words of command following all the preliminary measures which had already been put into action.

It had been known to the Colonel—Leslie Neilson— since the 19th (and two days later to all the men) that the Battalion was to move to Korea as part of a scratch British brigade numbered 27 and including the 1st Battalion of the Middlesex Regiment—and very little else. It was to reorganise on a special establishment designed for the type of country in which it would operate, and this in itself created a major upheaval within the Battalion. The habits of months (or perhaps years) had to be changed overnight, and those who formerly belonged to ' D ' and the ' Support ' Companies found themselves being rapidly disestablished. Three rifle companies and a headquarter company embracing all the supporting arms was the authorised way in which to fight this, the latest war—and no argument. Professional and personal disappointments there must have been, but all were swamped by the overwhelming feeling that now the months of strenuous training would be put to the test, and the Battalion would be given the chance to show its worth. Only Sergeant-Major Robertson, left behind for ill health after twenty-four years' service with the Regiment, was inconsolable.

Yet, in spite of this apparent reduction, the strength of the unit had been increased, for volunteers from the other regular battalions of the garrison had been marching in to swell the ranks. Thus it was that men of the Royal Leicestershire Regiment (traditionally known as ' Leesters ' in the Argylls) and the King's Own Scottish Borderers (or ' Kosbies ' to the Army) as well as the King's Shropshire Light Infantry and the South Staffordshire Regiment, found themselves among the first British troops engaged under the United Nations' flag against the Communists. (Among the odd things demonstrated by this peculiar campaign was the fact that the volunteer spirit is not yet dead ; and in proof of this, further drafts of volunteers from other regiments joined the Argylls from time to time.)

But even though these military adjustments could be settled satisfactorily, there still remained the individual human heartbreaks inseparable from any war. This regular battalion had left its wives and families behind a year ago and had gone abroad on an ' Emergency ' scale to a place that was a normal peace-time station. Events having proved that there was no immediate emergency, arrangements had been made for wives and families to follow. These plans were just about to materialise—indeed the women and children were already on the high seas—when their menfolk were ordered to Korea. This blow was philosophically accepted by the married soldiers as being one of the more unpleasant consequences of war, and to their credit it must be recorded that no consideration was either asked or expected. It was just one of the hazards of foreign service familiar to the Regular Army.

Was it fortune or foresight that a two-day brigade exercise involving the packing of all kit and equipment for

Plate 1a The Officers of the Battalion : *(left to right)* Captain John Slim (Adjt.), Major Kenneth Muir, Captain John Macdonald, Lieutenant Robin Fairrie, Lieutenant Ted Hunter, 2nd Lieutenant David Buchanan, 2nd Lieutenant Peter Mackellar, Lieutenant Owen Light, Lieutenant Mike Cawthorn, 2nd Lieutenant James Stirling, Lieutenant Crawford, 2nd Lieutenant Jock Edington, Captain Jock Haldane (M.O.), Captain Lloyd Davies (R.A.O.C.), Captain Neil Buchanan, Captain John Penman, Major Miles Marston, Major Jim Gillies, Major Ash

Plate 1b
Hong Kong : Detraining
before embarkation

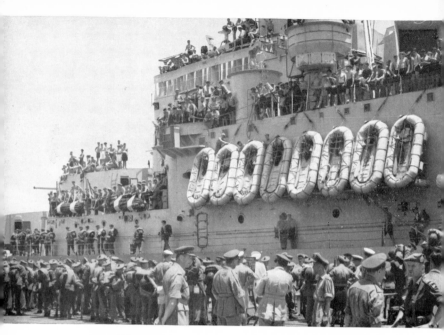

Plate 2a   Embarking in H.M.S. *Ceylon*, at Hong Kong

Plate 2b   Major Kenneth Muir, second in command of the Battalion,
is welcomed at Pusan

an operational move had just finished ? Whichever it was,
it caused a timely rehearsal which greatly eased the strain
of the days before embarkation. Thus all the loading
arrangements in H.M.S. *Ceylon* went smoothly, and with the
active aid of that ship's company, were completed by
Thursday night, 24th August. This day was in fact ' D–1,'
and H.R.H. The Princess Elizabeth sent a farewell message
to her 1st Battalion which was read out to all on parade.
This was the first war in which any battalion of her own
Regiment had been engaged since she assumed her appoint-
ment of Colonel-in-Chief, and her interest in its fortunes
was a real and living thing, that was evidenced in various
ways throughout its brief campaign.

On the same day, General Sir John Harding, the Commander-in-Chief of the Far East Forces, said a purposeful
word of farewell to the Battalion ; so there may have been
some irreverent soldiers who felt that a ' Sales Talk ' for
U.N.O. by the High Commissioner for the Far East on the
dockside next day was in the nature of an anti-climax.
On the other hand, the embarkation in H.M.S. *Ceylon* went
faultlessly. The Royal Navy are the masters of improvisation, and the embarkation of a battalion 600 strong presents
no apparent difficulties to them.

Those who have experienced the sailors' reactions on
similar occasions will all agree that the thing is made to
appear ludicrously simple. There seems to be an existing
drill for it which is termed an ' evolution,' and the result
is that the soldier is literally ' taken out of his element and
put in his place.' The routine of Friday, 25th August, as
carried out by the ship's company of H.M.S. *Ceylon*, was a
perfect example of this system. Almost as soon as the
Battalion had reached Holt's Wharf, officers and men found
themselves stowed away in the ship's interior, allotted to
wardroom, gunroom, petty officers' mess and mess decks,
and made to feel they were the welcome guests of the ship's
company. Thus was laid the foundation of a very happy
comradeship. The simple sailors, knowing from their

experience on the China station that a feeling of insecurity is engendered in ' Pongos ' who find themselves with neither land nor whitewash in sight, made all the necessary allowances for their passengers. Certainly no soldiers ever had better hosts ; and once they had understood (' hauled in ') the basic English of naval vocabulary and time-keeping, they all felt that a life on the ocean wave, at any rate in decent weather, had much to commend it. Not that all the Jocks were strangers to the sea. Corporal Carmichael, for example, had served most of the 1939 war as a sailor ; and the Battalion may be said to have entered the Korean War when Sergeant Walker, Corporal Jones and Corporal Williams went for a pleasure cruise in H.M.S. *Jamaica* two months previously and became involved in bombardments and actions off the North Korean coast. Williams, in fact, could claim to be the first casualty as he was slightly wounded when a shore battery registered a hit on the ship.

And now, with the cheers of the Hong Kong friends almost drowning the Borderers' pipers, the 1st Battalion of the Argyll and Sutherland Highlanders sailed to join the United Nations forces in Korea.

Their ship sailed in company with the carrier H.M.S. *Unicorn* carrying Brigade Headquarters and the 1st Battalion of the Middlesex Regiment. The C.O., Douglas Reith, who was to be Brigade Major, and an advance party had remained on shore to fly the next day with the Brigade Commander, Brigadier B. A. Coad, D.S.O. Thus the command of the 1st Battalion during the voyage devolved upon Major Kenneth Muir, whose father had commanded it from 1923 to 1927.

The Royal Navy, largely because it has spent much of its time in carrying the Army away from its scenes of unsuccessful action, is prone to take a jaundiced view of operations on shore. Luckily the Army knows this, and was not altogether surprised when it was seriously suggested that there might not be room enough to land the Battalion in Pusan. Not that this suggestion was altogether fantastic ;

it was simply the expression of a practical—if pessimistic—point of view. The American and South Korean forces were at that time contained within a dangerously small perimeter around Pusan, and it appeared to be even money on evacuation—a well-known 'form horse' as far as the Royal Navy was concerned. So the voyage was conducted with regard to the possibility of trouble off Formosa, and the routine of darkening ship (under a full moon) was dutifully observed. This 'blackout' was trying for the soldiers in the warm southern waters, but the atmosphere improved as the ship went farther north and encountered cooling rain squalls. Yet, although it was admittedly a tight fit below decks, life on board H.M.S. *Ceylon* passed very pleasantly. The pipes and drums and the Marine band made music together ; the troops took their turn at learning to operate the 'Bazooka,' three of these American tank-busters having been lent for training purposes ; and cigarettes, beer and whisky were duty-free and therefore unbelievably cheap. A correspondent reported that 'Dimple Haig was 4d a large one, so we didn't do too badly' ; but the most remarkable fact, from a purely historical point of view, is that *Ceylon's* commanding officer, Captain Thring, ordered the Battalion's flag to be flown in addition to the White Ensign. This was more than just a pretty compliment ; it was the outward and visible sign of the comradeship which was rapidly developing within the ship. And though one is tempted to write that this action is 'unique in naval history,' it can be truthfully recorded that the sailors themselves couldn't think of another instance.

And so they came to the harbour of Pusan on Tuesday, 29th August. By some re-arrangement of plan, *Unicorn* carrying the Brigade Commander did not at once go alongside, and so the honour of being the first British troops to land fell to the Argylls. (A similar distinction had befallen the 2nd Battalion of the Regiment in 1914 at Boulogne, and they had also been brigaded with the Middlesex at the time.)

Thus it happened that the Jocks bore the full blast of the official welcome by the Republic of Korea. And it was an ear-splitting blast too ! An officer writing home about the departure from Hong Kong mentioned the ' bags of ballyhoo ' that attended it. But if that was ' ballyhoo,' there can be no single word to describe the scene at Pusan. There was flag-waving, cheering, singing, sirens, bells and all the other accompaniments of mass hysteria. There was an American Army Negro band to welcome them—and a South Korean choir and band giving a near-impressionistic rendering of ' God Save The King,' specially learned for the occasion. And to crown it all, Kenny Muir was presented with a bouquet by the smiling daughter of the Korean Public Relations Officer. However, recovering himself from this gracious attention, he made contact with Colonel Neilson to find out the orders. These were brief and simple, and amounted to getting off the ship and into a train with all the baggage, equipment and weapons, as soon as it could be done. The perimeter was being held by desperately tired American troops, and Brigadier Coad had realised from his quick look round that his ' Brigade ' would have to take the field at once, before its transport could be un-unloaded, even without its own artillery. There was no time for ' special indoctrination ' (a process invented and cherished by their allies), and so he decided to skip that (and a lot of other things) and ' march to the sound of the guns.'

This meant immediate action by the Jocks, and H.M.S. *Ceylon* was once again the scene of violent activity. The spirit of urgency had impressed itself not only on the soldiers, but on the sailors as well, so that they joined in with a will and turned the task into a combined operation. This voluntary effort of the ship's company was the spontaneous expression of giving a hand to a friend in need, and was enormously appreciated by the Battalion. None will ever forget it—nor the meal generously brewed up by the galley for them as soon as it was known that they would get nothing to eat on the train. But even though all the gear was unloaded on the quayside there was no means of transporting it to the station. It was simply a question of manhandling, and here again the ship's company fell in alongside the Jocks and shouldered whatever was wanted. They were (as you might have said) irresistible, and the fraternisation and farewells at the train were so intense that nobody would have been surprised to find a sailor in any section next morning. That it didn't happen can only have been due to the vigilance of those in authority ; for the personnel of *Ceylon*, though generally in favour of the United Nations' cause, were entirely enthusiastic about fighting the war alongside their Scottish friends. This naturally formed comradeship was publicly recognised and renewed by the Regiment some six months later when its own active service was over, but that is another story which must fall into its proper place in this narrative.

The horrors of the train journey are best forgotten. It was the Battalion's first and last experience of Korean railways, and the veterans agreed that this one touched bottom as far as Eastern troop trains were concerned. Opinion is unanimous that, had it not been for the persistent energy of the company commanders who took turns at rousing the engine driver, the train would never have reached its destination. It appears that this key man did not take his duties very seriously, and tended to make frequent and unscheduled halts so that he might sleep by the railwayside —a pastime from which Majors Gillies and Gordon-Ingram with difficulty recalled him to his duty. It seems he took a poor view of the conduct of the war.

When this nightmare journey ended, the Battalion found itself allotted a ' harbour ' area near Kyongsan where 27th Brigade was concentrating, and here it remained till 3rd September, during which time its transport joined it by road. This was the first of many remarkable feats performed by these elderly vehicles and carriers which had needed repairs in Hong Kong, yet never received them throughout the brief campaign. But this time they brought with them a bonus in the form of several American Army drivers who at once established themselves on the Battalion's strength. Somehow they acquired Regimental badges, and in so doing identified themselves quite firmly with that ' kilt-wearing, proud Scottish regular-army organisation ' (Saturday *Evening Post*). No doubt, like every good American from the President downwards, each of them had a Scots grandmother. By 3rd September the 27th Brigade was placed under command of the 1st U.S. Cavalry Division and had moved farther west to the area of Taegu. Action could not be far off now, and the new maps with the outlandish names were earnestly studied by officers and men while guessing the next move. Then, on 4th September, they were ordered to relieve the 3/23rd U.S. Infantry Regiment, and found themselves on the east bank of the broad Naktong River, with the enemy on the other bank and also to the south of their own position.

From now onwards the reader will find the word ' Gook ' is frequently used to denote the enemy. The reason for this is to be found in the derivation of the word itself which was part of a greeting used to the troops by friendly South Koreans. They would smile and say something that sounded like ' Me Gook ' ; and so the Jocks took them literally, i.e. ' he says he's a Gook, so we call him one.' Then later, by a curious transposition of ideas, it became a synonym for the enemy, while the friendly South Koreans became known as ' Rok ' (Republic of Korea) troops. But they, although problematical, were not such a prevalent factor in the soldier's life as the North Korean enemy—the Gook.

Plate 3 (*Above*) 'Buy British !'—A Demonstration to the Americans of the Bren Gun : (*from left to right*) Private Duthen, Private Long, Private Orton, Private Morrison. (*Below*) 'On the Net': Battalion signallers making contact (Private Buttons and Private McEwan)

Plate 4 (*Above*) Erecting a shelter tent near Taegu. (*Below*) Taking a break
(Private John McKay and Sergeant George Morrison)

CHAPTER II

IN ACTION

THE position which the Battalion now occupied was said to be a quiet sector of the perimeter. This was true as far as lack of shell-fire was concerned ; and even mortar-fire, though frequent, could hardly be described as heavy. But the fortnight they spent there before crossing the river was invaluable to officers and men alike, for it accustomed them to the peculiar conditions of this campaign, and gave them their first experience of the Gook (or local enemy) and his tactical habits. It also saw their first battle casualties.

What was this strange land of Korea like ? Nobody in the Battalion had ever given it a thought until the necessity to fight in it arose. Even then, battered and dusty as they found it, it did not seem worth a second thought. However, those of us who were not there would like to visualise the scene of this latest war, so that we can see the Argylls in action against a proper background. Even so, it is not easy to come by an explicit description of the scenery, but one who had travelled far and wide in the service of his country, both in the last war and since it ended, has recorded his impression that it was ' a strange mixture of Kashmir, Baluchistan and a bit of the Arakan.' In this southern part the hills are quite high, rising to about 2,000 feet, although on the first position beside the Naktong they were little more than 1,200 feet. The same writer goes on to say that these hills ' are bare on the north and east slopes, with vegetation and pine trees on the south and west, and sometimes the cover is really quite thick.' There are little stone villages in the valleys, shaded by poplar trees and enriched by apple orchards, with rice-paddy fields terraced up the lower slopes of the hills.[1]

[1] An additional series of landscape targets may well be in print by now, for all the author knows !

There must be many who think that, because it was a Regular battalion, it was a unit composed of hardened veterans of the 1939 war and therefore well able to take the field with confidence in itself. This was (happily) the impression created in the minds of the Allied journalists by the appearance of all ranks, and by their behaviour in the field. But the fact is that comparatively few had seen any active service, and the Battalion had not fought as a unit since leaving Palestine in 1948. Even in the intervening two years its personnel had changed considerably, and you might say that the officers above the rank of captain, and the warrant officers and sergeants, were its only battle-tried components. Still, it was encouraging to know that your Allies thought you were a lot better than that, and the Scottish chest protruded a lot further in consequence. The great Napoleon had a maxim about the relation of the moral to the physical factor in war, from which no doubt has come our indiscriminate use of the French word ' morale.' He would have found confirmation of his ideas had he seen the regiment that guarded him in St Helena arrayed for the Korean war. They were fighting on a strange establishment, in a discouraging country and in an unpopular war. Their transport was decrepit, their equipment was not the most modern, and they could not even call on their own artillery for support. But—and here Napoleon would have smiled —they had trained, and trained hard, with that same equipment under leaders they knew and trusted ; they were an old regiment with an honoured name ; and, most essential, they were the only Scots in Korea. And so, fully alive to the situation and with that glorious self-confidence that belongs to a well-trained and well-led team, the Jocks took the field as for an International at Wembley, conscious of the eyes of the world upon them. From now onwards, every report about them, both in bad times and better times, emphasised this spirit by including the phrase ' the men are in good heart.' And that was nothing less than the truth.

The real trouble about this first position was the 6,000

yards gap in the so-called perimeter to the south of the
Battalion, between them and the nearest American unit.
This called for a routine of active patrolling to the south
to find out the enemy strength in that area, if necessary
by fighting. Such a patrol set off on the afternoon of
6th September under command of Captain Neil Buchanan.
They duly drew the fire they expected and split into two
parties. The fire increased, thus disclosing the strength and
disposition of the enemy. And as the fire was returned by
the patrol, and the small-scale but uneven battle developed,
it became clear to Buchanan that his little party had accom-
plished their task and ought to get back with their information. His sergeant (Walker) was wounded, as well as three
other men (volunteers from the Leicesters), and he himself
rendered incapable of being moved except with great
danger to his comrades. In these circumstances he properly
ordered his men to withdraw and leave him behind. This
order had to be repeated before it was reluctantly obeyed,
and the patrol slowly withdrew, leaving him where he lay,
and his batman, Private Taylor, wounded beside him.
This was the last the men saw of either of them, and later
attempts to find them failed.

Colonel Neilson, however, though reporting them as
' missing,' was always convinced they were dead and not
prisoners. In this he was proved right, for some months
later, when the tide of war had flowed beyond it, their
graves were found at that spot by an officer whom he had
sent to search there. This patrol action cost the Battalion
a total of seven casualties in killed and wounded, and was
on that account unfortunate. Yet nobody had expected
the campaign to be easy, and it was generally realised that
there would be more hard lessons to be learned before it
was over. And so experience of the Gook and his methods
was gradually gained by means of day and night patrols
into his area. Sometimes this meant crossing, or attempting
to cross, the Naktong River which was about a hundred yards
wide on the west front of the Battalion. On one such occasion

Captain Penman took a patrol down to the river bank by
night, intending to cross in a small assault boat. When they
launched this contraption they soon found that it could
not be controlled because the current was too strong, so
Penman decided to leave his patrol on the bank in position
to cover him, and swam across with his batman Mitchell.
Though they were both strong swimmers (Mitchell held the
Royal Humane Society's certificate) it was as much as they
could do to reach the opposite shore. In fact the current
caught hold of Mitchell's Sten gun, which was slung round
his neck and resting on his shoulders, and pulled the weapon
right round to the front so that it was dragging him down.
A nasty moment ; but grabbing a hand from Penman he
managed to land, and after completing their reconnaissance
they both swam back safely.

The Battalion's position, each of the three companies
stuck on hills overlooking (and overlooked by) the Gook
across the river or to the south, offered few comforts. The
most forward company was about 2,000 yards from the
enemy positions in the hills to the south, and 1,000 yards
from the strongly defended ' Orchard area ' across the
river. It was so forward indeed as to be almost isolated.
There were no roads or even tracks into its position ; rations
had to be manhandled by a coolie path, and so it was
arranged to drop ice to save the weight of carrying water
cans ! Its casualties were evacuated by helicopter, providentially the day before the heavy rain fell and caused
flooding. The only ' road ' ran parallel with the river bank
and therefore in full view of the Gook, so it was not much
use except at night. It therefore required caution. One of
the Battalion jeeps was overturned on it in daylight by
enemy fire, and its occupants with some difficulty were
rescued by the indefatigable firm of ' Penman & Mitchell.'
After which, even more caution was required.

So for a fortnight the Battalion sat in its slit trenches
(American ' foxholes '), learning by patrolling and observation what sort of enemy they were fighting, and how best to

avoid the effects of his mortar-fire. It was here that the
Jocks won their first 'home' fixture against the Gooks,·
and it happened like this. At 3 o'clock one morning a
strong enemy patrol vigorously attacked a machine-gun
section, and though it was driven off it was not before it
had inflicted casualties. Next day it was arranged that this
machine-gun section should, after dark, move to another
position, this time inside 'A' Company's defended locality.
This was done, and that night Sergeant Morrison took out
a patrol which duly reported an enemy party on the way.
Everyone was alert, and sure enough the Gooks again
attacked the former machine-gun position and found it
empty. Here was the perfect situation for which the Jocks
were waiting. The enemy was within their lines and would
have to get out again somehow before light. One of the
platoon localities was bound to be attacked ; and No. 1
Platoon under Sergeant Robertson, being on the homeward
route, was the one that was selected. Forty-five minutes
after the blank attack—minutes packed with suspense for
every man in the company—the Gooks cut the telephone
line and attacked No. 1 Platoon with grenades. Normally
this sudden rupture of the silent night would have been the
cue for a violent outburst of firing and Verey lights. But
that was not the way Robertson proposed to deal with the
intruders, knowing very well that night-firing is normally
ninety per cent inaccurate. Not one man fired in reply,
and the platoon position remained undisclosed. In this
curious silence his company commander spoke to him on
the radio and asked what was the situation. Robertson
briefly reported that there was a large enemy patrol round
his position, and that he was just waiting for enough light
to see to shoot and then he would 'let them have it.' In a
few minutes' time, he did so. The result exceeded all
expectations. The Gooks broke and fled with panic-
stricken yells, not waiting to fire their weapons in reply,
and leaving ten dead upon the ground. No 1. Platoon had
no casualties. Scotland's first victory.

And what of the enemy ? The Gooks had never been encountered before by the British Army, and all that was known to the Jocks was that they had rolled back the R.O.K. (South Korean) divisions very rapidly, in spite of the assistance given by such American formations as had managed to reach the line and stiffen the Pusan perimeter. So the Gook had to be judged on his performance, which in turn had to be measured against something known—some accepted standard. An experienced company commander who had fought with the 2nd Battalion (the 93rd) in Malaya made the following comparison between the Korean and the Japanese. ' He is not unlike the Japanese in his habits, but I would say he was about 33 per cent as good by day, and only 50 per cent as good by night. I have seen quite a lot of his movements by day (we never saw a Jap though) ; and his positions, though good and well concealed, are nothing like as good as the Jap positions. Nor does he stay in them till the last man—which is lucky for us. But nevertheless he can fight very bravely indeed. Of course we have not seen the original North Korean who was probably very well trained, and the chaps we have been up against are the third-line reinforcements.' All of which goes to show that the Battalion was opposed by tough Asiatic fighters operating in their own country and heartened by initial successes, a sufficiently formidable opposition for the early stages of a campaign.

But now the tide of war was turning in favour of the tenuous but stout-hearted Allies who had held the perimeter for so long. Their ' build-up ' had now reached the point when large-scale offensive action could be carried out, and plans for crossing the Naktong River in force and driving the enemy westwards were being formed. The original scheme allotted the honour of being first across the water to the Argylls, who were to be the leading unit of the whole 8th Army. However, as on other occasions, the familiar cry of ' It's all changed ' was soon heard ringing around, and the 27th Brigade was ordered to cross the river lower down and then protect the left flank of the American advance on Songju. As far as the Battalion was concerned, that meant the usual sordid journey in trucks over mis-named roads to their next sector and crossing-place. But it also meant an unopposed crossing, although a certain amount of harassing shell-fire accompanied them across the rickety pontoon foot-bridge which the Yanks had managed to erect. This shelling apparently came from the direct fire of a roving self-propelled (S.P.) gun, and continued to give trouble to all who made the river passage, being especially troublesome to the vehicles which were interminably crossing on an improvised mechanical ferry that not infrequently failed. Quarter-master 'Dodger' Brown and the men of the 'B' Echelon did a really successful job there, not only in getting the vehicles across, but in keeping the Battalion supplied during the critical days in that area. They did not often get into the news, and never had the satisfaction of dealing a blow at the enemy ; but the men in front of them, though free with the traditional jokes about those in the rear, were nevertheless equally free in admitting that they faithfully delivered the goods. The old maxim of Army maintenance says that the fighting soldier should never have to turn his back to get anything he needs—in other words, the chain of supply is from rear to front. Though this is often difficult of accomplishment, the good unit Q.M. will drive himself and his team to the limit of endurance to ensure that the system operates. In this respect the Argylls continued to be fortunate throughout the campaign—whichever way they were going !

The 27th Brigade was now on an 'Axis,' that is, they were operating on a second-class road. The hills here were much higher and thickly covered with fir trees, presenting good defensive positions for the enemy, and it was plain to Brigadier Coad that the high ground on either side of the road would have to be cleared before the Brigade could resume its advance on Songju. He made his plan accordingly, but had some difficulty in extracting from his

Divisional Commander any artillery support, as the Americans believed the hills were not held and the enemy was retreating in considerable disorder. However, on 22nd September the Middlesex attacked the hill on the right of the road, found it occupied, but captured it with surprisingly few casualties after a sharp fight. But it was now after midday, and the Argylls had little enough time and daylight left in which to capture the hill on the left of the road—the other part of the Brigade plan. So Colonel Neilson modified his orders and sent 'A' Company under Major Wilson to occupy an intermediate position from which 'B' and 'C' Companies could be supported in their attack on Hill 282 (the main objective) later that afternoon.

So at 14.15 hours 'A' Company left their assembly position and marched off, well extended, down the road to the accompaniment of some desultory shelling. Considering that the enemy enjoyed unhampered observation of this road it is lucky that nothing fell near enough to cause damage, though the 'near misses' were sufficiently unpleasant. This was the preliminary phase of the first Battalion attack that had been attempted, and all were keyed up to show their Allies what proper tactical training could do ; so David Wilson took advantage of the proximity of the Reconnaissance Company of the 24th U.S. Cavalry Division to arrange for some co-operation from their tanks. It turned out that their commander, though only rated a 'master sergeant,' was a first-class soldier who had been an Air Force captain in the last war, and on being shown the route and objectives, agreed to do whatever was required. Thus, as soon as the enemy were sighted on or near the objective, accurate tank fire was opened and 'A' Company walked unopposed on to the position and dug in, having suffered no casualites. And so the opening phase of the attack was quickly and neatly concluded and protection ensured for the start-line of the main attack.

Back at Battalion H.Q. Colonel Neilson was pleased with the success of this minor operation, but realised that day-

Plate 5   Private John Madden digging in

Plate 6   Harvesting with the Korean 'A' frame (Lance-Corporal Bell and Corporal Stoner)

light was not going to last long enough to enable the artillery
supporting his main attack to register their defensive fire
tasks after Hill 282 had been captured. He therefore
obtained permission to delay his next stroke until early the
following morning. No violent enemy activity followed
' A ' Company's action, and the night was quiet. There
was nothing more that the attacking companies could do.
They had moved forward to a ' lying-up position ' ; they
had all seen their objective by daylight, and knew their
orders thoroughly. For them there was only that burden
of uneasy sleep that comes to all men before a ' set-piece '
battle, but which bears hardest upon the young and untried
soldiers, of whom there were many. Preparations for their
dawn attack timed for 05.15 hours on 23rd September were
now complete.

It was just before dawn that the watchful men of ' A '
Company heard the other two companies forming up in the
dry river bed below Hill 282. Then, as it grew lighter, they
were able to see the leading platoons of ' B ' Company commanded by Lieutenant Mackellar and Sergeant O'Sullivan
launch themselves up the hill to make contact with the
enemy. It was a difficult scramble too, pricking their way
through the densely planted fir trees and among the loose
rocks that covered the precipitous slope. It was not the
easiest country in which to maintain direction in the half-
light, and though a certain intermixture of platoons and
companies inevitably occurred, it was all sorted out on
arrival at the top. But speed and surprise were the main
features of this attack, and in just under one hour's climbing
the two forward platoons of ' B ' Company were on their
objective and jumping on the necks of a large enemy breakfast party who were completely taken by surprise. There
was much confused firing in which both platoon commanders were wounded; but, lying on the ground, Mackellar
and O'Sullivan cheered their men on as, led by Corporal
Sweeney, they routed the enemy by a proper Highland
charge, and drove them downhill. It was a sharp and

successful engagement, in which fifteen enemy dead were counted on the position, while other 'runners' were seen to be hard hit and to fall and lie still on their way down the reverse slope.

But it was not the whole garrison that was caught at breakfast. In their zeal to reach the top, the leading platoons had unwittingly bypassed another bunch of Gooks who opened fire on Company H.Q. and No. 5 Platoon as they climbed. The did not enjoy their superiority for long. Second Lieutenant David Buchanan led his men straight at them up the steep slope and, entrenched and determined though they were, turned them out of their trenches. Thus in just under one hour the Argylls had captured their objective with a loss of twelve casualties. The secret was the old military principle of surprise, in this case produced by speed and determined leadership.

By this time 'C' Company under Major Gillies was on the position, and reorganisation began. Notwithstanding this easy win in the first round, Major Gordon-Ingram commanding 'B' Company was quite alive to the possibility of a counter-attack which would almost certainly come through his own area rather than that of the other company. Though they had gained their allotted objective, it now appeared that this was only a part of Hill 282, and was in fact overlooked by a higher feature on their left front. Not a secure position by any means, and least of all for Lieutenant Edington's No. 7 Platoon of 'C' Company, which found itself (owing to a miscalculation in the dark advance up the hill) the nearest one to the enemy in the other company's area. Not that it mattered much, for Gillies and Gordon-Ingram, who were organising their position, decided that the most important thing was for everyone to dig in at once so as to be ready for any counter-stroke ; and that when that had been done, they could be ready for the next advance to the higher hill on the left. This eminently sensible decision was shortly to be proved right— if indeed proof was needed. Meanwhile digging started on hastily sited defensive localities ; and at the same time they began to get the casualties down from the hill. This proved a very difficult job, for anyone who could not walk had to be assisted down the steep and rocky hillside ; and the men of 'C' Company, being at the moment farther from the enemy than the others, were engaged in this task. This made them 'a bit thin on the ground' (as Jim Gillies described it), and when you think that the hill was about 900 feet high, you will realise that it took over an hour to bring a casualty downhill and then rejoin your section on the top. In fact, when about 08.00 hours the expected shelling and mortaring began and caused more casualties, it was realised that this was a case for the Battalion stretcher bearers, and they were called for on the 'blower.'

About the same time, two other things happened which directly influenced the later course of events that day. First Jock Edington, nearest to the danger, reported that the enemy were trying to 'infiltrate' from that high feature on his left front ; and then both the forward observation officers of the supporting American artillery were withdrawn by their regiment. It was the most unexpected and dangerous thing that could have happened at that moment, for there was the enemy counter-attack developing, and the small British force with no adequate means of breaking up this advance at long range. Leslie Neilson at his Tactical H.Q. was assailed 'on the air' by both protesting company commanders, but when he spoke to his brigadier he found that all artillery support had been withdrawn by orders from the Division H.Q. There was nothing he could do about it, since he knew that the tank guns, though willing to help, were quite useless because of the lie of the land. An unpleasant predicament for a commanding officer who sees his men isolated in face of the enemy and can do little to support them.

But something else was happening on Hill 282 of which he was unaware. As the expected attack on No. 7 Platoon developed so the gaps in Jock Edington's ranks widened,

and Alastair Gordon-Ingram decided that the platoon must
be reinforced if that vital position was to be held. Both its
commander and his sergeant were wounded, and there were
so many other casualties that the platoon had virtually
lost its identity as a fighting unit. Buchanan was therefore
ordered to take his men forward and plug the holes, and
for two more hours they fought off the enemy. It was no
light task, for they were taking punishment all the time, as
the dense undergrowth in front of them made it easy for
the Gooks to approach unseen to within a few yards of
this sitting target and fire their ' Burp ' guns. Towards
11 o'clock, Gordon-Ingram realised that this unequal contest
must be stopped. The platoon could no longer effectively
withstand this relentless attack unsupported, and must now
come within the main defended area of the company. The
necessary orders were given, and Buchanan skilfully withdrew the remnant of his platoon, still holding the enemy
at bay.

It was about this moment that a breath of fresh air
reached the small fighting force, and a party of stretcher
bearers (including some Middlesex volunteers) led by the
second-in-command, Major Muir, arrived on the hill. Here
at any rate was practical help, and a chance of speeding the
wounded down to the dressing station—a vital necessity
since no morphia was available. Sergeant-Major Collett
who had been working the system of evacuation, now seized
thankfully on these new helpers and organised the dressing,
carrying and checking of the wounded. Kenny Muir, on
the other hand, found himself the senior officer in a rather
confused situation, with numerous casualties, and a strong
enemy attack developing. As Neilson's ' second ' he should,
in principle, have been back at the main Battalion H.Q.
whilst his C.O. was away with a Tactical H.Q. But you
cannot always go by the book, and here Kenny agreed with
the late Marshal Foch that it was a case of ' To Hell with
principles ! What's the problem ? '

The problem was to hold the crest ; but with ammuni-

tion running low and casualties increasing, the best method
was not so obvious. One thing was clear to him and that
was that he himself ought to stay there and take command
of the situation. This was his own personal decision, and
Leslie Neilson has recorded that when Muir reported that
he was up there he was glad of it. So Muir set about the
business of re-organising the two companies into one force,
making fresh dispositions, and centralising the collection of
ammunition from the casualties and its re-distribution to the
firing line. In this he was helped by a comparative lull in
the enemy activity, during which he called on the radio
for fire from the tanks to break up the enemy concentrations
which had been observed on the downward slope to the left.
The tanks responded, but from their position their guns,
which were not designed for this kind of fire support, could
not hit the target. The danger on the flank therefore continued unchecked. Muir then spoke to his colonel on the
radio and agreed with him that since artillery support was
non-existent and tank support ineffective, an air ' strike '
on the high ridge held by the enemy 1,500 yards to the
left was the only alternative. Though it could not hit
those actually attacking, it might well discourage others,
and strike a severe blow at reserves moving up to the attack.

So it was arranged. The ' recognition panels ' were put
out, so that the U.S. Air Force could distinguish their
position, and Muir's force set about repulsing the enemy
with their own weapons until the air strike could materialise.
Muir himself was the mainspring of the defence and was
universally recognised as such. Survivors have written that
' he was literally everywhere ' which is proof enough that
his personality impressed itself upon every man of his small
and dwindling command. Wherever the need lay, there
was the short, square-shouldered figure in a Balmoral to be
seen encouraging the men by voice and example, helping
the wounded, distributing the ammunition and directing the
fire. Regardless of personal safety, he had so warmed up
the defence that in the opinion of both Gordon-Ingram

and Gillies the tide had turned in their favour, and the situation was once more well in hand. All were now confident that the hill could be held, and indeed there were even signs that the enemy had had enough and was starting to withdraw. This was about 12.15, and shortly afterwards the sound of approaching aeroplanes was heard. The hearts of the defenders leaped up as the promised air support sailed into view—and then it came. Circling round, apparently to make sure of their target, the three Mustangs each made a ' run-in,' dropped a Napalm bomb and followed this by a machine-gun attack right on the Argylls' position. The whole surprising tragedy was over in two minutes, leaving the top of the hill a sea of fire which threatened to destroy both fit and wounded alike. The ridge became quite untenable ; the irreplaceable reserve ammunition was exploding everywhere in the flames, and the majority of the defenders were forced to escape the fire by plunging down the sheer slope. These, in fact, were unable to take any further part in the battle, because by the time they reached the top again the action was over. Down below, both the Commanding Officer and his Tactical H.Q., as well as ' A ' Company from their defended locality, were impotent witnesses of this dreadful debacle [1] ; but they were also proud spectators of the action taken to restore the situation.

On the flaming hill-top Muir, Gordon-Ingram, Penman, Sergeant-Major Murray and such others as had not been wounded in the air attack, withdrew to the lower ridge still occupied by ' C ' Company H.Q. There is no doubt that a complete retreat from the hill would have been justified at this time, and permission was given for this. But Muir, whose mind was still on the battle, watched the flames die down and then was able to observe that not only had the enemy failed to take immediate advantage of the situation and occupy the top, but that a small sector of it was still being defended by the wounded Private Watt and

[1] ' A ' Company in fact attracted a low-flying attack to itself.

come along with your boys—they're just O.K. for us and we like 'em ' ; and even an unsuitable offer of marriage ! But in spite of all the inevitable ' Ballyhoo ' that was let loose at the time—a natural indication that the general trend of events right along the Allied front was at last favourable—the Battalion's stock was built up high on a solid foundation of achievement. They had been admired for their appearance and their morale : they were now respected for their technical ability and their fighting quality.

Within his own H.Q. Leslie Neilson sat down to estimate his losses in officers, men and equipment, reorganise his Battalion on a two-company basis pending the arrival of reinforcements which were just about to join, and get ready for the next task, whatever it might be. In addition, he had to collect reports of the action from his company commanders, make recommendations for awards, and, at the first opportunity, keep the Colonel of the Regiment informed of the situation. It was at the end of a long letter to General Macmillan describing the action of 23rd September that he summarised the state of the Battalion by writing : ' In spite of it all, the men are still in tremendous heart.' And that, of course, was what mattered most.

The duties of a commanding officer in the field are many and various, and extend far beyond the professional business of leading his unit in action. Though the majority who read these pages will not need to be told that, there are certainly others who can have no idea of the scope of his responsibilities. His mind is always at work, dealing with the present, recording the past and planning the future ; and though he has a staff to assist him in carrying out his ideas, the decisions in most cases have to be made by himself alone. It was in the midst of all these activities that he was, at the request of the Colonel of the Regiment, already making arrangements for the collection of action reports, maps and photographs to be sent home for use in any future account of the operations, and was planning himself to write ' as soon as we are settled in more comfortable surroundings,' a skeleton outline of the campaign to serve as a basis for an historian of a later vintage. Had he not done so, I could never have attempted to write this book.

Meanwhile the transport drivers had been striving with unremitting labour to get the Battalion vehicles across the river, and at last on 24th September the temperamental ferry began working again, and Captain Youngson the transport officer was able to report that all ' wheels and tracks ' were on the right side of the water. Thus the Battalion, though weak in numbers, was once more ready to advance whenever required. Not that they were idle, even if they were for the moment stationary. The Brigade was protecting the left flank of a general advance by the Allies, and so care had to be taken that the advance was co-ordinated. This meant patrolling both in front and to the flanks, and on 25th an Argyll patrol made contact with the American troops advancing from the north-east, with the result that the following day the 27th Brigade was directed on Songju about ten miles along the road to the west.

This time supporting artillery had been put under command of the Brigadier, but no opposition was encountered, and Songju was ' occupied without incident,' according to the *War Diary*. Not an attractive place, it would seem, but the Battalion spent four days there engaged in ' mopping-up ' operations which involved chasing and rounding up the straggling North Koreans, and clearing mines. Hardly exciting, perhaps—just an ordinary infantry job. The enemy, in fact, were in a bad way and their formations were breaking up under the constant air and ground punishment being dealt out by the Allies. Individual Gooks (and even gangs of them) were zealous to throw away their weapons and uniforms, and to appear once more in the traditional white robe of the peaceful Korean country-man. It was in the course of this well-meant transformation that they were apprehended and put behind the wire. While engaged in this way Neilson received his promised reinforcements of officers and men, and so was able to form

Plate 7   Evacuation of Casualties from Hill 282 (the hill on the extreme left)

Plate 8   A Battle Casualty at Hill 282: (*left to right*) Private Syme, 2nd Lieutenant Edington (the casualty), (un-named) a Middlesex soldier ; (*in foreground*) Private Holmes, Private Mackie

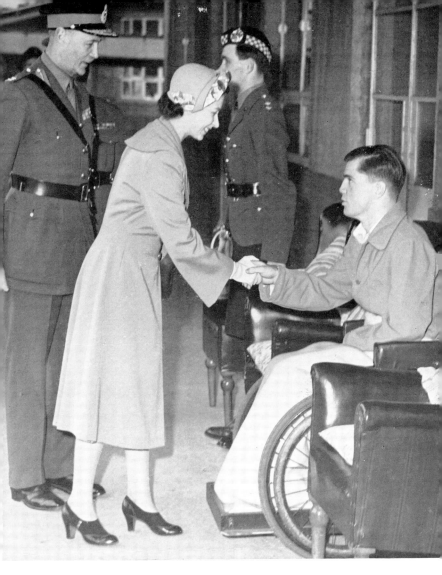

Plate 9   At Cowglen Hospital : H.R.H. Princess Elizabeth with Lieutenant-General Sir Gordon Macmillan talks to Lieutenant J. R. Edington

Plate 10 General Sir John Harding addressing the Battalion at Kassong

once more his third rifle company. This was a great weight
off his mind as his command was in an unbalanced state,
and if required to fight would have been like a man fighting
with both hands but on his knees. Some of these newcomers
included volunteers from other regiments, and though no
doubt on the way up to the line they had been given an
exaggerated idea of the prestige enjoyed by the Argylls in
the theatre of war, it is interesting to note that their first
reaction on joining confirmed what they had been told.
A young lance-corporal from the Gordons in Germany
wrote :

> ' I have managed to get with the mortars. I had to
> give up my stripe, and believe me I was glad to. This is
> no place for green soldiers like me to take the lead, it's a
> job for the old soldiers and we have many of them.
> ' The mortar teams here are red-hot and know their
> stuff. It's a pleasure to be with them and it's a grand
> platoon.'

And that, generally speaking, was the impression that
the Battalion as a unit continued to make on all and sundry
throughout the campaign.

It was while 27th Brigade was in this area that it was
joined on 30th September by the 3rd Battalion of the
Royal Australian Regiment, and therefore proudly re-named
itself ' The 27th British Commonwealth Brigade.' Though
it did not as yet possess its own supporting arms, it was at
least three battalions strong, and its commander was enjoying justifiable hopes of an increase in the Commonwealth
component before long. The Australian accession of
strength was very welcome, and served to redress the tactical
balance of the Brigade. Indeed, it would appear from
what immediately followed that the American Commanding
General was only waiting for their arrival to start the Brigade
on a series of forward moves which did not cease till the
end of October. The first of these was the relief of an

American battalion at Kumchon by the Argylls, and their own relief by the Australians, thus giving the Brigade a wider area of responsibility. But that was only a beginning, for on 4th October a warning order was received for the Brigade to move to a concentration area somewhere north of Seoul, and preparations were at once started. It was to be rather a complicated move in two echelons, the men by air and the vehicles and stores by road over a distance of roughly 150 miles, and the Colonel was to go on ahead of the Battalion to plan future operations under the Brigadier. The pursuit had begun, and the enemy was to be kept on the run and chased back across the 38th Parallel (that obscure geographical boundary), or perhaps even farther. Everybody's tail was well up, because, as Mr Winston Churchill has sagely observed in *The Hinge of Fate*, ' there is no doubt that people like winning very much.'

CHAPTER III

' ON, ON ! '

THE apparently complicated move ended with complete success, and all parts of the Battalion were reunited (with gratified surprise) at Kumpo airfield (just east of Seoul) by 5th October. The air travellers appear to have had the best of it, as they had four days rest at their destination ; and were certainly envied by those who had driven and ' harboured ' along the dusty Korean routes. Though its authorship is obscure, it is probable that some of the road party compiled ' The Stooge's Guide to Korea,' which is here reprinted, with acknowledgments to its unknown authors :

Harbour area—A windswept area of frozen paddi occupied by shivering troops.

Brew up—A tin of ' C ' rations, or an abandoned vehicle surrounded by a large fire.

Main supply route—A column of vehicles, nose to tail, incapable of forward or backward movement. (See Convoy—Traffic jam.)

Fire missions—A stern sermon by the Padre on one's probable future existence.

Harbour party—A disorganised collection of officers (N.C.O.s) drivers and vehicles, who should have been ready to leave half an hour before they were detailed.

Transportation—Not applicable to 1st A. & S.H.

Successful patrol—Return of any body of men with a supply of pig, fowl, firewood, brew cans and Gook bedding.

Convoy (Traffic jam)—The terms are the same in this theatre, and represent the opposite of ' perpetual motion.'

At any rate, its basis was bitter experience, even if hard Fact was overcoloured by Fancy !

Once concentrated and ready for action, the next move was a short one to the area of Kaesong where the Commonwealth Brigade came under the command of the 1st U.S. Cavalry Division for the general advance northwards which was expected to follow the battle for the 38th Parallel, at that moment being waged. This would mean carrying the war into the enemy's country, and at the risk of being labelled 'Aggressors' it was the considered military policy of the United Nations to take this step. The Battalion, having no political views, welcomed the decision but deplored the inactivity which kept the whole Brigade in the Kaesong area for a week with no immediate prospect of action. However, it was during this week that General Sir John Harding visited the Brigade, and as the Battalion was the only unit of it which was conveniently concentrated and available, the Commander-in-Chief addressed the officers and men as representing all their comrades. Soldiers are like the rest of us inasmuch as they always appreciate a word of praise for a job well done—even if that job was simply 'all in the day's work.' And, like the rest of us, they prefer the word of praise to be short and to the point. Having heard the Commander-in-Chief on the Hong Kong quayside the Jocks knew what to expect—and they were not disappointed. There was no formality, and they simply gathered round in the open while he addressed them standing on an upturned box. These were his words, which were later printed and circulated to the absent units of the Commonwealth Brigade.

'All ranks of the Argylls, I want to congratulate you most warmly on what you have achieved since you have been here.

'What I have to say is to be regarded as being addressed to the Brigade as a whole. I congratulate the Argylls and the Diehards. You remember when I said goodbye to you in Hong Kong I said that the honour and reputation of the British Army and the British people rested in your

hands. You have maintained that reputation and maintained it very well indeed.

Well done the Argylls !
Well done the Diehards !
Well done 27 Brigade !

' I have heard personally from your Brigadier of the
operations in which ' B ' and ' C ' Companies of the
Argylls were engaged on the 23rd of September. I was
most deeply impressed with the courage and endurance
with which you attacked the enemy, the heroism with
which you accepted the casualties you suffered and the
energy and gallantry with which you returned to the
attack. That engagement reflects the very greatest credit
on you. I feel extremely proud of you and the people at
home will be proud of you too.'

They served to show that the Brigade, under-strength and
under-equipped though it was, had justified the decision to
send it ahead as a British token of the support which was
later to be given to the United Nations. And though at this
time it was not made public, the Commander-in-Chief told
the Brigadier and Commanding Officers that it was intended
to return the Brigade to Hong Kong in the near future once
the 29th Brigade had taken the field. (This formation was a
fully equipped one which was coming from the United
Kingdom and was intended to be the basis of the main
British contribution to the campaign, whereas the 27th
Brigade had only been meant for a ' stop-gap ' role.) It
was a comforting bit of news for Neilson, who had begun to
wonder what would happen to them if winter suddenly
descended, as well it might, now that they were so far to
the north. They had embarked in tropical kit, and proper
clothing for a winter in those latitudes was non-existent as
far as he knew. Even his normal clothing replacements of
boots, socks, shirts and headgear came from American

sources of supply, and he could only hope that if his Battalion was caught out in the cold before being removed to Hong Kong, the American ' G-4 ' Branch of the staff would not forget their inadequately clothed Allies !

It was quite soon after they had taken the field that he had, with prudent forethought, forbidden the men to wear Balmorals and badges, realising that although their value as souvenirs would be out of all proportion to their price in the ' Ordnance Vocabulary of Stores,' they were quite impossible to replace. Therefore the knitted ' stocking cap ' became the standard wear from an early stage of the campaign, as will be seen in many of the illustrations to this book.[1]

Of course it was inevitable that ever since the Battalion landed it had been flooded with publicity, first by the Press correspondents who had travelled with it from Hong Kong, and then by those already with the American Army. There was no news censorship, and in many ways this was a good thing, though it had its disadvantages. It was, for instance, a matter for great regret that highly coloured news stories of the action on Hill 282 together with names of casualties should have been allowed to appear in the British newspapers at home before the next-of-kin could be officially informed. This was only the result of serving under American Command and therefore under a different code of rules ; but the system was adjusted as far as British troops were affected, when once it had been properly represented in the highest quarters, and no further cause for complaint occurred. On the other hand, the arrival of the Jocks occasioned some remarkably funny items in the papers for those who were lucky enough to see them, and three at least seem worthy of preservation. One paragraph was headed quite seriously : ' Anglo-British co-operation at the front-line level has been close.' To which *Punch* appended, ' How about the Argylls ? ' Another (not so seriously) recorded that the pipers had

---

[1] Curiously enough the steel helmet was not worn by the British troops in this theatre.

landed in Korea, and reminded its readers of the difficulty that a North Korean would experience in trying to keep his hands above his head while stopping his ears ! But it was left to an American journalist to write a fresh chapter of Regimental history in these words :

> ' In the Crimean War of 1855 they created a legend in history when the 93rd Argyll Regiment charged into the face of Russian artillery at Balaclava. School children to-day know them as the " Thin Red Line "—the six hundred who rode into the Valley of Death. Tennyson immortalised them in his " Charge of the Light Brigade." '

Unfortunately there was a serious lack of newspapers from home—except for those that were sent to lucky individuals—and when this had been reported to the Colonel of the Regiment, he arranged for this shortage to be made good through the Public Relations Branch of Scottish Command. A month later newspapers began to arrive with some sort of regularity, and all began to feel more in touch with the things they had known and loved.

It is this business of ' keeping in touch ' that does so much towards building up the heart of the fighting man in a distant land. Much as he appreciates good recreational facilities, canteens, shower baths and the other things that are rather loosely classed today as ' Welfare,' these are universal and therefore impersonal. It is the steady flow of letters from home to front and back again that preserves his individuality by retaining in his mind the picture of the life to which he hopes to return. Somehow it became apparent that there was a weak link in this important chain of communication ; and though letters from home were arriving as frequently as could be expected, having regard to current operations, those from the front were clearly taking an unduly long time between the army post office and the individual. If officers lead the men, their wives must lead the women ; and so it was Mrs Gordon-Ingram at home who took the first effective step to remedy this by representing it to the Member for Argyll, Major Duncan MacCallum. No better champion could have been chosen, for he, having been a Regular officer himself, attacked the problem with vigour and tenacity, finally raising it in the House of Commons. As the result of his efforts the root of the trouble was found and eradicated, and the system was operating satisfactorily by the end of the year.

But the week of inaction soon passed in the expectation of better things, for had not the Brigadier himself promised them they would be given a ' proper axis ' for the next advance ? Yet it was an unexciting start, for it was the Middlesex and the Australians that pushed north-westwards into the hills to do the work, while the Jocks went along the road netting the Gooks that had been flushed by the drive on the high ground. And then the weather broke. Down came the rain, and down came the temperature with such suddenness as to make everyone think that winter was already on their heels though October was but half-way through. ' Nice weather for the ducks ' they would have said at home—but they would have been wrong. Into his tent that night where the Commanding Officer was trying to get some sleep before an early move the next morning, came a squad of ducks. Roused and wrathful he drove them forth. But it was no good ; apparently it was too wet outside, even for ducks, and they returned to remain muttering mutinously to themselves all night. Not that they were strangers in any way—far from it. They belonged to that essential element of Battalion H.Q. in the field known as ' meat on the hoof,' an all-embracing term. And with the dawn they were handed back to their competent military authority, i.e. the sergeant cook.

The next morning, 17th October, saw the Battalion ' spearheading ' (as the saying went) for Sariwon, the local Aldershot. Although nothing was known of the enemy, speed was the essence of the thing, and ' A ' Company under Major Wilson was in the lead, mounted on tanks and

Plate 11 (*Above*) 'A' Company in action at Sariwon, 17th October 1950
(*Below*) The Gook and the Jock : The Private and his Prisoner at Hung-so-ri

Plate 12   Reinforcements leaving by air, September 1950, from Lyneham, Wiltshire

in lorries. Under his command was a comprehensive collection of supporting weapons—some British, some American—that must have reminded him of the opening situation in a 'tactical exercise without troops,' but with the addition of a 'liaison' aeroplane, an unforeseen refinement of modern warfare. They had about thirty miles to cover that day so the advance started at 6.40 a.m. with No. 1 Platoon, under 2nd Lieutenant L. B. Cunningham, sitting astride Shermans. In spite of delaying action by snipers in two villages, the column maintained a decent rate of advance until it was about four miles out from Sariwon. Here the road ran round a bend, and the real opposition in the shape of anti-tank guns and automatics was met, and No. 1 Platoon was in action. David Wilson, moving in his jeep a hundred yards or so behind his leading troops, was able to observe the enemy deserting an orchard on the left of the road, and quickly directed the fire of the nearest tank on to them. Simultaneously, with the aid of his radio, he committed his other two platoons—one to attack to the left and the other to cover it from the right—and told his mortars and machine guns to fire in support.

'At this moment' (in his own words) 'the Liaison aircraft which had been flying ahead of the column chose to land in front of my tank thus impeding further progress down the road, and there then developed a gap of 800 yards between myself and my leading platoon into which the Press and visiting generals rapidly infiltrated. This did not aid the general conduct of the battle.'

Nevertheless, the fire plan was so straightforward, and No. 2 Platoon (under 2nd Lieutenant Light) attacked with such terrific speed within its protection, that the enemy never attempted to fight back. They abandoned their well-prepared positions and ten machine guns, leaving about fifty dead on the field. There were few casualties in 'A' Company, and the road into Sariwon was now open for the

Brigade. It was a neat, workmanlike fight, the sort that is normally referred to in military literature as an ' Encounter Battle.' Yet, intelligent as the Press are about these things, there were many of their representatives filling up David Wilson's road-space who thought it a waste of time and energy and a piece of British exhibitionism. They considered that the correct procedure would have been to have gone on ' barrelling down the road ' (*à l'américaine*), and that a ' setpiece attack ' was simply mounted in order to demonstrate British tactical training. A novel idea, and one which still leaves unexplained how otherwise does an advanced guard leave the way open and safe for those whom it protects.

It was now 4 o'clock in the afternoon, and the Brigadier was anxious to clear the town and consolidate his position. This was when the fun really began ! ' B ' and ' C ' Companies were to move through the town (which had already been bombed by the Air Force) and clear the main axis of advance, while the Australian Battalion passed through the Argylls and occupied an area north of the town. Alastair Gordon-Ingram, looking back from his jeep to make sure that ' B ' Company was behind him, found he was being followed by the same pack of ' Press and visiting Generals ' that had so impeded David Wilson's conduct of the battle !

Gracefully accepting this unsolicited ' Advisory Committee ' as one of the minor horrors of war, he drove on with his Company into the town, where he was to organise a Battalion strong-point, while ' C ' Company went on to the northern outskirts, and the Australians through them again, and on to block the road from the north. Apart from sniping there was little to worry about—though the sniping was heavy and continuous. But the Brigadier was beginning to be concerned with the possibility of the enemy being driven into the town from the south-west owing to the advance of the 24th Division on that flank, so he told Neilson to put one Company in a suitable position for blocking that road. The Colonel collected his reconnaissance party in their two vehicles—himself, Sloane, the second-in-command, Mitchell representing ' C ' Company, and his escort. They drove into the town and were about to turn left at the road junction when they met a lorry-load of North Koreans who had just come into Sariwon from the south. Events now began to move rapidly. The enemy saw their mistake and opened fire. So did ' B ' Company, and the snipers (and probably the ' Advisory Committee ' too) for never had there been seen such a volume of small-arms fire in such a confined space.

Gordon Ingram was standing behind his jeep picking them off with his revolver and looking exactly like the sheriff in an old-time ' Western.' Everybody was enjoying it—except the C.O.'s party who were caught between two fires, and had to bale out and run for cover with bullets whipping the air all round them. However, once they had a wall between themselves and the Gooks in the lorry, they too joined in the volley firing, though Neilson's Sten gun jammed and gave him a red face for a moment. But not for long ; an impatient Jock suddenly heaved a grenade into the vehicle and brought the battle to an end. After this interlude which cost the Argylls nothing, Neilson took his party off on their interrupted mission down the road. The light was fading by then, and they suddenly found themselves motoring between two columns going in the opposite direction on each side of the road. Neilson had recognised them at once and told his driver to step on the gas. The leading Gooks (for such they were) opened fire, but luckily there was no reply, for he estimated the enemy strength at 2,000. Then, inexplicably, there was no more firing, and for four miles they drove on through this involuntary march-past until they had cleared the column. Gasping with relief at their extraordinary luck, they turned off the road, abandoned their vehicles and spent a comfortless night in a ditch doing ' two on and four off ' until daybreak.

On their return to the Battalion in Sariwon they heard

the rest of the story which was equally fantastic. The 2,000 Gooks they had encountered were retreating from the U.S. 24th Division in the south and approaching Sariwon in complete ignorance of the fact that it was occupied by the Allies. In the town they only saw the Jocks in their stocking caps looking strictly un-regimental, so they were still unenlightened. As it happened, the men they saw were the Mortar Platoon under Lieutenant Robin Fairrie, withdrawing through the street from the north to another position. Surprise was mutual ; but the Gooks made the first move by addressing the internationally hatted Jocks interrogatively as ' Russky ' ? Affirmative Scottish noises were made in reply, but almost at once it dawned on Fairrie and his boys that here was a delicate tactical situation. However, they maintained the deception with assurance while cigarettes and backchat were exchanged. Robin Fairrie, in fact, was issued with a North Korean comfort girl as a passenger in his Jeep, who at once cemented international relations by exchanging hats with him. And then somehow the deception failed and the shooting started and all was chaos for a few moments. Nobody quite knew the cause, though the *Saturday Evening Post* correspondent attributed it to an incautious American who came on the scene and had not witnessed the preliminaries. When addressed as ' Russky ? ' he replied ' Hell, no ! '—and that was when things began to go gay. But whatever the cause, the result was that the Jocks were left scatheless in the street, while the Gooks left their dead and streaked out of the town to the north, only to be captured or killed by the Australians !

It only remains to be added that Robin Fairrie, with some difficulty, succeeded in recovering his Balmoral, as his unwanted passenger had leaped out of the Jeep during the mêlée and vanished.

Thus ended a most unorthodox day, even for this most peculiar of wars.

The Battalion earned great praise from the Commanding General of the 1st Cavalry Division for their rapid advance

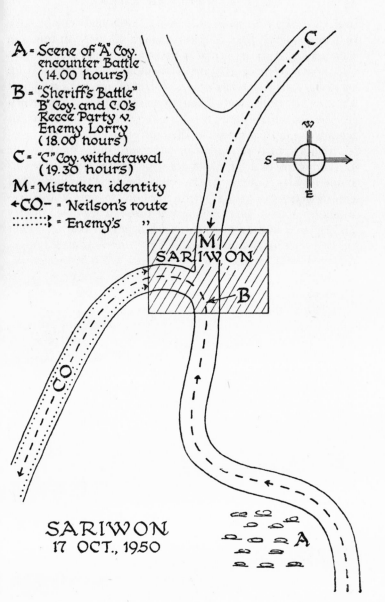

A = Scene of "A" Coy. encounter Battle (14.00 hours)

B = "Sheriff's Battle" "B" Coy. and C.O's Recce Party v. Enemy Lorry (18.00 hours)

C = "C" Coy. withdrawal (19.30 hours)

M = Mistaken identity

←C.O.– = Neilson's route

::::::::} = Enemy's   "

SARIWON

SARIWON
17 OCT., 1950

41

and capture of Sariwon, which was reckoned an objective of some worth. But, pleased though he was at this, the Colonel could not let it pass without a characteristic military comment. Writing a report of the action he summed it up by saying, ' It was really only a matter of pressing on against little or no resistance.' And that, of course, is confirmed by the fact that the same Company was able to act as advanced guard throughout the entire march.

The capture of Sariwon, however, only marked the beginning of that phase of the operations which gives its name to this chapter. There was to be no sitting down and counting the score ; the enemy was on the run, and it was intended to keep him moving fast through his own country and squeeze him up against the Manchurian border. Thus tired company commanders, hoping for a peaceful night and a day of ' make and mend ' after a tactical advance, would be roused by the Colonel on the blower with the ominous words ' We're continuing the advance tomorrow. On, on ! ' Still, even if it was exhausting it was also exhilarating to be going in the right direction. They were moving through the rolling plains now, and were soon in Pyongyang the enemy capital. The Allied Air Force and artillery was harassing the retreating Gooks by day and night, and with nothing but hastily organised opposition against them, the advance of the Commonwealth Brigade was only limited by the lack of a good road. The whole district seemed to be remarkably full of barracks and police stations, and apart from its general similarity to Salisbury Plain, an impression grew that this must have been one of the North Korean military training areas. As far as the Jocks were concerned it had rather less attraction than any training area they had ever used, and simply none of the amenities. It was just another slice of this unfriendly and comfortless country in which they waged the United Nations' war.

At Pyongyang the Brigadier fully expected a rest for his men. But no ; the orders were to change to another division but keep on in the lead and make for the ' MacArthur Line.'

(This was a strategic line beyond which the Higher Command had decided that the United Nations would not advance except in certain circumstances.) And so, in spite of minor opposition, the forward movement continued. There was a somewhat sticky night in front of Yong-Yu where 187 Airborne Regiment (dropped three days previously) were fighting furiously. 'A' Company lost three men on the fringe of it, and Wilson was told to burn the town next day on account of the sniper menace to the advance. This he gladly and efficiently undertook, and when the conflagration was going nicely he was ordered to put it out as the gunners couldn't get their limbers through on account of the heat !

Next objective was Sinanju on the banks of the Chongchong River. Here the enemy managed to impose a slight check on the pursuit. The Battalion was in the van that day and had covered twenty miles in order to secure the crossings of the Chongchong River for the Brigade. The river reached the west coast at this point and divided itself into two estuaries, with a bit of solid ground between them. A quick look at the land from the hill to the east of the town showed that the bridges over both estuaries had been blown, and movement drew some light artillery and machine-gun fire from the farther bank. This was stopped by an air strike, and the American engineers began to explore the possibilities of repairing the bridges. But it was no use ; they were beyond repair, and so they built a pontoon bridge a little farther upstream in less than forty-eight hours, over which the Middlesex men crossed on 25th, easily overcoming the light opposition from the ground between the estuaries. The Jocks and Australians followed unopposed. But the Gooks still held the high ground on the northern bank, and on 26th the Australians and the Argylls set out to dislodge them.

They crossed the northern estuary (with the aid of a pontoon bridge and the local yachtsmen) and gained their objective with little trouble. It seemed as though the enemy had no intention of offering more than a token resistance on this natural line of defence, and heightened the general opinion that the end of hostilities was almost in sight. It was with a sense of elation therefore that the Brigade, never pausing and still leading the advance, sped northwards to Pakchon. Here the general bearing of the pursuit changed from north to west, and the Brigade was directed on Chongju about thirty miles away. The first obstacle was the Taenyong River, and it fell to the Australians as leading battalion to cross it and secure a bridgehead. They did it—but surprisingly, they had to fight hard for their success, and it was clear that the rest of the Brigade would not be able to follow until this tenuous foothold was strengthened. So the Argylls pushed on a little farther north and crossed the river on tanks with the object of taking the hills west of Pakchon and establishing a second bridgehead. This was a job for ' B ' and ' C ' Companies, who successfully achieved their purpose against slight opposition and with the minimum of casualties. By nightfall they had relieved the right-hand Australian company, and both bridgeheads had not only been increased in depth but linked together. That action allowed the remainder of the Brigade to cross, but did not entirely dispose of the opposition on that front, for the Middlesex in their advance on 27th had to fight another sharp battle in the hills a little farther to the west.

The last two days' fighting gave a foretaste of the quality of resistance to be encountered on the rest of the way to Chongju. It was the general opinion that it was higher than had been met at any time since the offensive began on the Naktong River, and the advance next day was therefore carried out slowly and thoroughly. The Argylls led it, the foremost platoon mounted on tanks, the remainder of its company a few hundred yards behind, and the Battalion itself less than a mile astern of its leading elements. Time was taken to clear all likely enemy positions and thus secure the Brigade's route. The air support was invaluable and knocked out five tanks in front of the leading company, as well as helping the infantry to deal with minor opposition, and the result was that it was rather late in the afternoon by the time the Battalion was within striking distance of Chongju. The Commanding Officer, knowing full well the significance of this, reported the situation and was ordered to stand fast and dig in where he was. There was not much daylight left, and a further advance at that late hour, in the Brigadier's opinion, might have involved them in a battle at quite the most tactically inconvenient time of day.

Events on the morrow were to prove him right. There was some shelling that night, thus indicating that the enemy was aware of his danger, and early the next morning the Australians passed through on their way to take the town. Sure enough, it was no 'push-over'; they had a day-long fight for it against the fiercest enemy yet encountered, and the town of Chongju was absolutely flattened by the end of it. But the Australians had won; and the Argylls with due acknowledgment to the victors, crossed the Taechon River next day and entered the remains of Chongju virtually unopposed. On that, the Commonwealth Brigade stood fast and an American Regimental Combat team passed through. It marked the limit of their advance westward throughout the campaign, and they were justifiably proud of themselves for they had been continuously in the lead for the past two weeks. It had been a stupendous effort for this 'scratch' formation which had been obliged to beg not only its supporting weapons but its transport vehicles from every division in which it served. Not that this support and assistance had ever been withheld; only that it made the plans so much more complicated than they would have been had the Commonwealth Brigade been self-contained.

And now, at the end of their triumphant progress, they suffered two losses. The officer on whom the burden of the staff work naturally fell was the Brigade major, Douglas Reith. During the advance on Chongju, the 'command vehicle' in which he was travelling had to pass a stationary convoy on a narrow road, and in doing so the bank gave way under it and it fell fifty feet. Reith, still talking on his radio set, was imprisoned beyond escape and died from his injuries. It was such an unnecessary fate to meet in the course of active service, and the Regiment and the Brigade alike mourned the loss of an able officer who had filled a difficult and responsible post with considerable ability. His place was taken by Major James Stewart, an Argyll officer of great experience and proved capability who had flown out with the reinforcements. The other blow that fell in this moment of victory struck the 3rd Battalion of the Royal Australian Regiment. During the day that followed its successful assault on the positions defending Chongju there had been some desultory shelling, and by the greatest misfortune a shell landed in Colonel Green's headquarters and mortally wounded him. An officer who had served with a distinguished record in the last war,[1] he had been given command of this picked Battalion of volunteers for Korea, and had led it with such skill and determination during its first month of operations that its name already stood high. Nor was it ever held in any lower estimation after his death, for it was undoubtedly a good battalion.

After this battle the slogan ' On, on ! ' ceased to be heard, and the Brigade's advance to the north stood still within twelve miles of the Yalu River and the mountains of Manchuria. All enemy resistance on that front had been overcome, and the Brigade enjoyed on 31st October the first day of rest which it had known since the 17th October. There was ' make and mend,' cleaning up and sorting out among the units, as well as welcome issues of ' goodies ' from the beneficent ' PX ' (Post Exchange). As far as the Jocks were concerned, they had won this uncomfortable war and anyone was welcome to keep Korea. But the Intelligence Summaries which filtered into Brigade H.Q. told a different tale that indicated a troubled future. For the first time in the campaign, the presence of Chinese ' volunteer ' units on other fronts was definitely confirmed.

[1] In the Byron Regiment, affiliated to the Argyll and Sutherland Highlanders

CHAPTER IV

WINTER WITHDRAWAL

THE general feeling of the Battalion was that they had done well, that they deserved a rest in reserve, and would probably get one. This was a reasonable enough assumption if the result of the pursuit had been to strike a final and damaging blow to the North Koreans, which seemed likely in view of General Douglas MacArthur's statement that his troops would be ' home for Christmas.' Yet, although they could not at that time know it, the entire strategical situation had undergone a radical change within forty-eight hours of the end of their triumphant chase. The arrival from Manchuria of Chinese Communist formations, politically referred to as ' volunteers,' had temporarily shifted the balance of man-power in the theatre. Providentially air supremacy still belonged to the United Nations, though the latest trend of events gave some cause for wondering how long this might endure. The general uncertainty of the situation first manifested itself by the Battalion ' harbour party' being sent for at 11 o'clock on the morning of 1st November. After that it became clear that local affairs had taken a different turn, because the Battalion found itself motoring back over its old battlefield and finishing up near the scene of ' B ' and ' C ' Companies' action on 26th October in the hills west of Pakchon.

Here they bivouacked next to the Headquarters of the 24th Division—and found it blacked out. But the tales of the Chinese entry into the war had begun to circulate, and the dull mutter of the flashless guns to the north confirmed them. It was a crisp, cold night with a rising moon, and an almost tangible feeling of suspense over the whole camp. The *War Diary* observes laconically, ' A protracted rest seemed most unlikely,' and goes on to record that ' the

47

C.O. went to Brigade H.Q. for orders.' There he found that the Brigade was to move up north to Taechon and occupy a ' holding' position whilst all around them were performing a south-easterly withdrawal. Not without difficulty, the Battalion with its American tanks under command was in its new position by 3 p.m. on 2nd November; but an hour later Neilson was at Brigade H.Q. and was told that they would be moving, probably that night, to Sunchon, south of Sinanju on the Chongchong River which they had crossed less than a fortnight ago. A disheartening prospect; and though it didn't happen that night, the Battalion eventually found itself as far south as Sunchon before the end of the month.

Meanwhile, together with the Middlesex, the Battalion remained with its chin stuck out at Taechon, facing roughly east and south to cover the approaches to the town, but with orders to go back to Pakchon (whither the ' harbour party' had already gone) whenever the troop-carrying transport arrived, which was supposed to be at about 2 p.m. Neilson was far from happy about his situation. Though not in contact with the enemy, air reports placed them within four or five miles of him to north, east and south-east; moreover, the nearest Allied troops seemed to be twenty-five miles away. In the circumstances the enemy seemed to be too many and too close; nor was it quite clear what the two battalions would be able to accomplish, if seriously attacked. This he tactfully represented to his superior. Evidently the Brigadier's information was much the same as Neilson's, for he gave permission for both battalions to withdraw to Pakchon at once, and this they did about noon on 3rd November using tanks and artillery vehicles to supplement the lorries. About forty minutes after the tail of the column had cleared Taechon the enemy entered the town.

This was the situation which caused the newspaper correspondents to report that the 27th Brigade had been cut off and obliged to fight its way out! Neilson hastened to correct this report by saying (as Mark Twain did about a report of his death) that it was ' exaggerated,' and that they had not been cut off ' but only a little delayed.' The withdrawal was, in point of fact, unopposed, and the Australians were found to be holding the important cross-road at Kasan on their route. By the time the Argylls reached their new position they found two pleasant surprises. The first was their own ' harbour party ' which had travelled as far south as Sunchon and then been turned back ; the second was their ration truck which had gone adrift on the previous night and had consequently been given up for lost. This adventurous vehicle had wandered far outside the Allied perimeter and had visited both Kusong and Chongju without penalty. These fortunate re-unions were followed by a quiet night—blessings which were much appreciated after the vicissitudes of the past forty-eight hours.

It is not my intention to weary the non-military reader with the constant change of plans and orders which were, inevitably in the circumstances, the frequent lot of the fighting soldier during the course of this withdrawal. It is always the same in every campaign when the enemy has the initiative and is thus, to a certain extent, able to dictate the course of events—and the ultimate effect on the fighting man is always the same. The orders change as fast as they reach him, and it cannot be denied that a sense of uncertainty and disquietude is engendered which tends to unsettle officers and men alike. The fact that in this case the Common-wealth Brigade was fighting under American Command was not the cause of the confusion. It simply made the circum-stances a little bit more difficult because the Brigade was not yet self-contained. Therefore I hope the reader will bear this in mind throughout the narrative of these dark days, and will understand that there was frequently this background of constant change and consequent confusion, though it is not invariably mentioned.

Pakchon looked much the same as when they had passed through it a week previously. The sandbag bridge to the north of the village was still there, and capable of taking

vehicles ; but the crossing with which the Battalion was to
concern itself this time was the damaged bridge to the south
In spite of all the efforts made to repair it, this was only
passable for men on foot.   However, only ' A ' Company
which had an independent role of guarding the road to the
bridge over the Chongchong to the south of the Battalion
was required to cross that night.   The remainder stayed on
the west bank opposite Pakchon in a defensive perimeter
Patrols by day and night for the next twenty-four hour
reported no contact with the enemy, and it was not until
early on the morning of 5th November that the expected
enemy attack developed.   The first news was that they
had penetrated the American position on the right of the
Commonwealth Brigade during the night, and by 8 a.m. it
was obvious that there was further enemy activity on the
other flank.   Mortar bombs were exploding near the main
road to the south, and there also seemed to be considerable
quantities of white phosphorus bursting in that direction.   As seen by Battalion H.Q., this appeared to be an
attempt to destroy the bridge over the Chongchong and cut
the main road to the south, thus isolating the Brigade
There was no attack on the two companies facing west, so
Colonel Neilson at once ordered them to cross the broken
bridge and launch a counter-attack in support of ' A '
Company.   Though this would leave the high ground west
of the river unoccupied, he accepted the risk in the absence
of enemy activity on his immediate front—and indeed it is
difficult to see what else he could have done with only three
companies.

It was a long process moving the two companies across
that unstable feature truthfully referred to in reports as
' Broken bridge south of Pakchon.'   The men had to cross
it in single file, and well spread out to minimise the risk of
casualties, for there was a certain amount of desultory sniping going on.   It took about two hours altogether for the
crossing to be completed, and by 10 o'clock ' B ' Company
was formed up with its tanks and advancing to the scene

of battle. They had had a few men wounded coming over, including the Company Commander, ' Sheriff' Gordon-Ingram ; but Captain Penman, who had recovered from his wounds at Hill 282 and returned from Japan by an unorthodox method which had better not be described, took over command. Followed by ' C ' Company and supported by the Middlesex machine-gun fire, they forced the enemy to withdraw into the hills to the east of the main road, and stabilised the position. In the meanwhile, ' A ' Company with its supporting weapons had been ordered north again to where 61 Field Artillery Battalion had been engaged on its own since 8 a.m. in the battle which Neilson had observed from his headquarters.

Strongly resisting all invitations from excited Allies to join in a private battle which he could see to the north, Major Wilson had remained mindful of his orders to act as a ' backstop ' to counter enemy moves round the southern flank of the Brigade position. It was not until an American tank officer told him the orders were ' to attack the road block ' that he took action, and then only on orders from his Battalion Commander on the tank radio net. But, once having had them, he took his company off at top speed towards the enemy, mounted on tanks and any form of transport vehicle he could impress. (Even then he had to leave behind one section per platoon to guard his area and the two 17-pounder anti-tank guns which formed part of his force.)

The Company soon found out what was meant by the ' road block.' This was a euphemistic term for a battlefield which, when first seen, presented a spectacle reminiscent of a very much older war. ' C ' Battery of the 161 U.S. Field Artillery Battalion had been attacked by enemy who had infiltrated from the high ground on their right flank and were seriously threatening to overrun their gun lines. Thus challenged, the American gunners formed their guns in a circle and engaged the Chinese at point-blank range with these and any other weapons they could handle. As the men at the guns were hit, others came forward to take their places, and this was the inspiring sight that greeted 'A' Company. As the Jocks arrived the shooting died down, and it was seen that the enemy dead were lying only thirty yards from the gun shields.

In order to clear the road and keep it clear, Wilson decided to attack a small hill about 800 yards away on the east of the road. Leaving one platoon to hold a 'firm base' on the road, he launched the other two at his objective, supported by his four tanks, machine guns and mortars. (He could have no artillery support, for the gallant gunners were out of shells.) In twenty minutes the hill was theirs, and the supporting weapons were making great play among the Chinese on the far side of it. The time was now 10.30, and as the position appeared to be stabilised, part of the garrison on the hill was withdrawn to the road. Half an hour later the situation had deteriorated, and a counter-attack by large numbers of the enemy had driven the small force off this feature. Casualties were mounting and ammunition (especially for the tanks and mortars) was running low, though the machine guns under Corporal Campbell were still giving effective support. Wilson wisely decided not to try to retake the position as he would not be able to hold it with his depleted numbers, but to occupy with his reserve a nearby feature from which he could effectively prevent any further enemy advance, and thus secure the road which was his special responsibility. This he did successfully, and with the arrival of fresh ammunition 'A' Company was able to reduce enemy activity to the minimum and so, later, ensure the unopposed withdrawal of the Brigade down the road.

There had been two rather remarkable aspects of this brief action. The first was the extraordinary intensity of the air strikes which were delivered from time to time. They surpassed anything previously seen in this line, and greatly delighted the Jocks. The other was the discovery that the enemy possessed 1943 pattern Bren guns filled with 1942

Plate 13   'Music hath charms' : Pipe Corporal Pitkeathly and PFC. Herd

Plate 14   R.S.M. T. Boyde D.C.M.—' and friend '

ammunition. Wilson, who had defended Kohima in 1944, realised these weapons had been flown to the Chinese ' over the Hump ' at that time for a very different purpose. But the men of ' A ' Company cared nothing for speculation of that sort ; they simply took the weapons into use and asked no questions.

It had been a noisy 5th November, and the Company had lost 5 killed and 6 wounded in the short battle, though they estimated that the enemy had lost 200. There had been many individual acts of gallantry and devotion to duty contributing to the success of the day. For instance, there was Corporal Patterson who, though seriously wounded, refused to retire from his position ; Lance-Corporal Stark who lost his life saving a wounded comrade ; Sergeant Clarke killed whilst directing the invaluable fire of the mortars, and many another. They, and Corporal Campbell's machine gunners, will all be remembered for their part in displaying superior tactical skill against superior numerical strength.

Now that the road to the south was open again, the planned withdrawal of the Brigade continued through the Argylls' position, Battalion H.Q. being the last to move. By 3 p.m. the whole Brigade was back on the Chongchong River and facing north, its withdrawal uncomplicated by the enemy. A strong bridgehead was formed and they fully expected to be attacked ; nor were they disappointed for the Australians had to repel two attempts in the night. Nevertheless, nothing happened next day, and patrols went out as far as five miles without finding a trace of the enemy. A cautious and limited riposte was therefore successfully delivered in order to enlarge the bridgehead and make the position more secure. And then began a slow forward crawl to an area just north of Pakchon which lasted till 24th November but produced no clashes with the enemy. It was a matter of probing with patrols and making sure of each position before going on to the next. And it was the last advance for ten weeks. Winter weather had set in, and hopes of Hong Kong for Christmas were finally and officially abandoned. In spite of their own negligible northward movement, the general situation on the Allied front was far too unstable and unpredictable to allow any reduction of strength. Yet their release had been so near, and all were buoyed up by the thought of it. There had even been a sailing date—21st November—given.

How well one knows that feeling of hope which is kept alive in dark days by the prospect of something brighter. One has experienced it so often in the little things of life, that one can, even at this distance of time, sense the feeling of disappointment and frustration, the sinking of the spirit, which must have been engendered by the enforced abandonment of this almost tangible 'happy ending.' Yet, even deprived of this hope, there was no weakening of the determination to complete the job. It is the British soldiers' established privilege to grouse—and they exercised it. But those in command knew their men, and were still able truthfully to report them 'in good heart.' But there was also a practical problem posed by this indefinitely postponed departure date, for winter suddenly arrived one night with a north-east wind and twenty-five degrees of frost. The Battalion's vehicles, old as they were when they left Hong Kong, were not only older but less repairable now, and that hard frost played havoc with them, for several were found to be non-starters next morning with consequent damage. The devoted fitters worked ferociously on them and managed to get them all fit for service, but this sort of thing obviously could not endure for long.

Then again, there was the question of the clothing problem. Ordinary British battle-dress was no answer to a North Korean winter, and the 29th Brigade which had arrived in the country from the United Kingdom was properly equipped in every way for an Arctic campaign. But the Commonwealth Brigade who had been expecting to be relieved by them, now found themselves in a most unenviable position. They had to carry on the war, certainly into the winter and possibly beyond it, with this makeshift gear. However, it was not in vain that they depended upon the supply system of their American divisions, and soon the British units began to present a remarkably international appearance as articles of American winter clothing were issued. Windproof jackets and fur hats were certainly the most popular items, and the general opinion was that the British Ordnance Department had not produced anything as well designed to withstand that sort of weather. (It is just possible that there were some others, besides the Commanding Officer, who could remember the 2nd Battalion wearing fur caps on the Legation Guard in Peking some twenty years before, but to the vast majority this headgear was a magnificent innovation !) Another deservedly popular number was ' drawers, woollen, long,' an unusual issue for Highland Regiments ! These things, and the string ' under-shirt ' (well known to troops on ski-training in Austria) formed the basic winter uniform ; but Colonel Neilson at once realised that other woollen things generally classified as ' comforts ' could probably be sent out from home if only people knew that the Battalion was in need of them.

This idea reached the chairman of the Regimental Association, and Brigadier Clark lost no time in translating it into action. All members of his Committee and all Lords Lieutenant of the counties of the Regimental area were told about it ; a ' Comforts Fund ' was started, wool was bought in bulk and arrangements made with the War Office to send the parcels by air. At once every branch of the S.W.R.I. in the ' Regimental Counties ' began knitting socks and scarves and cardigans for dispatch through the depot at Stirling to the front ; and although this may break the chronology it must here be recorded that the first consignments reached the Battalion in January. These were doubly welcomed, not only for their own comforting sake, but for the knowledge they brought that those at home were thinking of them as they battled through the northern winter in the barren land. This woollen warmth was in fact the tangible expression of the goodwill which has always belonged to the Argylls in their own district, and as such it was recognised and enormously appreciated. Not only their bodies but their hearts too were warmed by the touch of this homely hand that had been stretched out half-way across the world.[1]

The stealthy edging forward, a few thousand yards every day, continued throughout the next two weeks. But it was not the enemy that was responsible for the creeping tempo of the advance, for the Brigade was hardly ever in contact with them. It was the necessity for conforming to the movements of the other Allied formations that dictated the speed. Thus it happened that they were stationary on Sunday, 12th November, and the Chaplain was able to conduct a short service at Battalion H.Q. and observe the two-minute silence. For many of them this was probably the most significant Remembrance Day service they had attended, for in its silence they were remembering not only those impersonal, nameless comrades of previous wars, but those who had so recently fought beside them. Reality and religion march hand in hand in the field, though not always in the paths of peace ; and the Padre could always be sure of a full congregation of the ' off-duty ' men whenever he conducted his short services in the Company positions.

During this comparatively static period there occurred that great American anniversary known as ' Thanksgiving Day.' This fell on 23rd November, and being under American Command and on the American ration strength, the Jocks were preparing to celebrate the occasion in a truly American manner and without any prejudice at all ! The omens were good : the ' R.O.K.' troops on the flank had ceased firing their weapons so indiscriminately that the Battalion got the ' overs ' ; the Brigade was due to go into Corps Reserve ; and the turkeys actually came up with the

[1] The ' Comforts Fund ' bought £500 worth of wool and dispatched 750-lb. weight of ' comforts ' with the donations it received. And the Girl Guides and Brownies of Stirlingshire made a mass response to a request from the Battalion for handkerchiefs.

rations ! The cooks got down to them at once, and in fact spent the entire day trying to deal with this delicacy. The trouble was that the birds were frozen so hard and stiff that they simply couldn't be cooked at all ! And so another piece of joyful anticipation went wrong. However, it was only a case of ' hope deferred,' and they were all able to enjoy a proper ' Thanksgiving Dinner ' next day, thanks in this case being given to the cooks who had to put in a lot of overtime in its preparation. This was the day that the planned offensive towards the Yalu River began, and the Commonwealth Brigade went into Corps Reserve. The offensive did not go too well, but the Battalion made the most of its few quiet days before the general withdrawal began to produce the inevitable repercussions. They had a concert party from 24th Division, they had a cinema show, and—best of all—a system of baths for the Brigade was initiated. About a hundred men had a hot shower each day ; and though it may sound incongruous to record it of this, the latest and most modern of wars, this was the first piece of real comfort they had enjoyed since they crossed the Naktong two months ago, for it was the first time that the majority of men had the chance to get fresh clothes !

These few days of rest and relaxation were welcomed by weary warriors, and the Jocks made the most of them, being totally unable to foretell when, in the course of this crazy and uncomfortable campaign, they might get another chance. Not for some little time, it would seem, to judge from the Commanding Officer's news on returning from Brigade H.Q. on the night of 26th November. The ' ROKS ' and the Yanks were falling back on either flank of the Corps, and the Reserve looked like being required. At any rate, the ' Order Group ' followed by the Battalion was to go to IX Corps H.Q. at Kunnu-ri next day, and action looked imminent. Yet it did not materialise. Although Neilson was warned to be prepared for a number of eventualities, and the Battalion was packed up and at short notice for all of them, the morning of 28th November made it quite certain that the Brigade was bound for Sunchon to keep the main supply route open—the original task which had been allotted to them with the first change over to the defensive at the end of the pursuit to Chongju. Of course the orders were to move ' as soon as possible ' ; and of course this was another of those times when the troop-carrying transport failed to arrive. This time the hurry was so great that the Brigadier would not wait for it, but simply said, ' The Brigade will march.' And the Battalion *War Diary* states quite simply : ' 13.45. The Bn. moved off with "A" Coy leading and the pipes playing.'

Taken out of its context, this typical piece of military understatement might give the impression of a Battalion route march at home ; but in fact it was a rather more harassing march than any soldier had ever undertaken in his training. There was a horrible feeling of uncertainty about the whole situation, and nothing but bad reports from the front. Did this intervention by the Chinese mean another rolling back of the Allied line and a further prolongation of the war in this wretched land ? How far was this place they were making for ? And was there any guarantee they would get there before the enemy ? It was beginning to look as though the British might be called upon to act as rearguard at Sunchon and see their Allies pass safely through them and down the main supply route to the south. These and similar doubts must have been in every soldier's mind as they marched through the frozen fields and along the cold dusty road, carrying whatever else they could handle extra to their arms and equipment. The last motor vehicle overtook and passed them ; firing was heard ahead ; the daylight died and they were on their own. In the gloom the hills appeared more sinister, the valleys more forbidding ; and all were uncomfortably conscious of being watched by an unseen enemy. (The Middlesex in fact fought an action along that road next morning.)

Halts were regulated by David Wilson on his hunting-horn, and its clear notes could be heard echoing down the glens—a challenge and a warning to their foes. The Jocks themselves used to refer to this performance afterwards, with cynical exaggeration, as ' The Death March ' ; but observers saw nothing to support this ! Each company had its own pipers, and as they trudged down the North Korean road to the tunes their fathers had known, they must have thought of home. All music evokes memories ; but surely the pipes must be its most nostalgic form ! It was a Scottish officer far from his own regiment who had wished for just that music as he trekked through the Burmese jungle :

> Oh for the piper striding towards the morning,
> Half-hidden in the gloom,
> Playing my choice—
>   ' Steamboat,' ' The Gypsy's Warning,'
> ' The Wee Man at the Loom.'

Thus they marched, company by company in open file on either side of the road, with intervals of fifty yards between platoons. And if the piper wearied, they sang songs—their own songs of home. A wise man once said, ' Let me make the ballads, and who will may make the laws of a nation.' If this be true, the late Sir Harry Lauder must rank as an Elder Statesman. They were ' in good heart,' and determined to prove what they had always firmly maintained, that they at least were capable of marching, even if some of their Allies had to depend entirely upon motors. It was 10 o'clock that night before the transport picked them up ; they had covered eighteen miles, but there was still a further twelve to go, and it was 2 o'clock on the following morning before all were safe in the harbour area.

The carriers had tailed along behind the marching column and had acted as a sort of rearguard ; and as the early darkness fell that wintry night, they brought the information that the rate of marching would have to be maintained as the enemy could be distinctly heard following up only a few miles behind. This news applied a spur to the weary ones, and Sergeant-Major Murray whipping in the laggards of the rearmost company was heard to observe,

' If you don't keep up with us, the next man you'll find coming down this road will be Joe Stalin.' Eventually the carriers ran out of petrol, and as they waited cautiously in the dark wondering whether the extra gas or the Gooks would reach them first, the sound of marching feet and men's voices approaching from the north finally settled the matter. It wasn't the Gooks—it was the Signal Platoon still plodding along the highway and unconsciously doing rearguard to the whole Battalion !

At Sunchon the situation was not much clearer. The Battalion was given a ' reserve ' role, and the usual reconnaissances were made and orders given for positions to be occupied, while at the same time the Commanding Officer was told to be ready for various other contingencies. One thing was absolutely certain, and that was that the withdrawal was in full spate. A ' vehicle patrol ' from ' B ' Company down the main road to Pyongyang only succeeded in getting caught up with a stream of motor transport all heading south as fast as it could go, and had to return ! It was certainly beginning to make a noise like the Commonwealth Brigade being last across the Parallel ! Even Pyongyang itself was abandoned by a sudden decision which took some of the rear services by surprise. A very efficient Indian Field Ambulance had joined the 27th Brigade by this time, whose able commanding officer was properly horrified at the prospect of being unable to take his valuable stores with him. Brigadier Coad told this story about him in a lecture about a year later.

' As soon as he realised that the town was going to be given up, he asked for a railway engine to pull his stores out. He was told that there was not one available, and that he must burn his stores. He said, " That is quite fantastic, because all my doctors will have nothing to do. We have six months' supply of everything." They then found an engine, but as there was no water in it the other ranks formed a chain and filled the engine up with

Plate 15 'The Death March' from Kunnu-ri. (*Above*) 'A' Company: (*in background*) Sergeant Coleman and Private Russell; (*in foreground*) Piper Scott, Piper Brown, Private Vearnals, Private Ireland, Private Cuthill, Private Stevenson, Corporal Stevenson, Private Kennedy. (*Below*) 'B' Company: Piper Craw, Piper McLellan, Private Russell, Private McNeil, Private Petty, Private Whitehouse

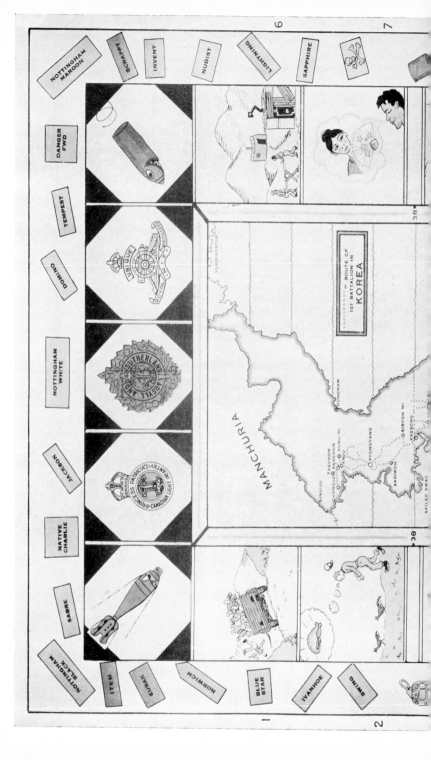

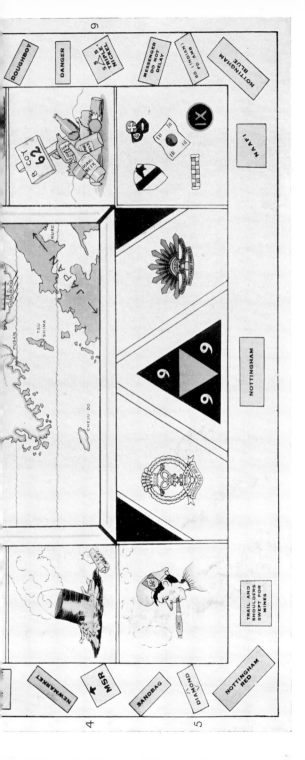

Plate 16   The Battalion coloured Christmas Card, 1951.

Key to inner Marginal Illustrations :   1 Road party ;   2 'Meat on the hoof' ;   3 'A'-frame load ;
4 Brew-up ;   5 'Goodies' from the P.X. ;   6 Shantytown ;   7 Leave in Japan ;   8 Lulu ;
9 Christmas at Ichon

Plate 17a 'Winter Woollies'
Private Jones washes his str
vest

Plate 17b
Spring comes to Korea :
Private Gethen on the look-

jerricans. Then they looked for coal, but there was no coal, so they went out wooding. They cut wood and lit a fire in the engine and got the water boiling. Two soldiers said they knew how to drive the engine, and they drove that train over the last bridge at Pyongyang at 04.00 hours in the morning. At 05.00 hours the bridge went up. It was a great piece of initiative and determination.'

The first three days of December found the Battalion acting in a detached role as a sort of flank-guard in the hills to the east of Unsan-Ni, where the 7th U.S. Cavalry Regiment had had a brush with the enemy a few days previously. The Battalion came under the command of Colonel Harris, the American Commander of Task Force 'Harris,' and the operation started by the Jocks marching across the frozen River Han while their transport crossed it lower down at a fast-flowing ford which was extremely difficult to negotiate. Just before dark, 'A' and 'B' Companies completed climbing the tallest mountain they had ever attempted (a Battalion record at that time), though this was not to be their final position. For this, they had to move farther to their left along the ridge they had scaled, and this they started to do on the morning of 2nd December. But soon after midday Colonel Neilson was told to stop their move and recall them to their original positions, because a further withdrawal to the south was contemplated. The general idea was for the whole force to pass through a bridgehead held by the Australians lower down the river, and in order to ensure the passage of the force a certain pass was to be held. This was the task of 'A' and 'B' Companies if they could be turned round in time and if the enemy (of whom little or nothing was known) were not already in occupation. Though the commander of 7th Cavalry wanted them in position by 5 p.m. with the last of the daylight, Colonel Neilson said it could not be done before 8 p.m. (This as it happened was an underestimate, but he knew full well the difficulties of the rough going in the hills, and the hazards of trying to take up a strange position at night which you have neither seen nor reconnoitred by day.) Orders for this change of plan were sent out to the two companies on the mountain and were, miraculously, received. It is said that the cries of despair of the senior officer ' up aloft ' were almost audible ; but what the men of ' A ' and ' B ' Companies said as they retired along the ridge while their bedding was being brought downhill by a carrying party of ' H.Q.' Company has never been recorded.

The remainder of the Battalion, with its carriers and some tanks, made for the pass by a track which was reported feasible. Fortunately the remaining transport had been sent right back across the river by the way it had come, for within half a mile of the start of this track it became so narrow that the leading tanks were wedged in it. At the tail of the column, six of the carriers had thrown their tracks, with the result that the way was blocked both front and rear. The leading tank had to be destroyed ; so also did some of the carriers ; and it took an hour and a half in the darkness to reverse the vehicles and get them back to the main road. An inauspicious start—but worse was to follow. The marching men continued down the dark and difficult track, and reached the appointed rendezvous in spite of heavy snow which had now begun to fall. ' A ' Company now went off the air, so no-one could be sure that Major Wilson and his two detached companies were holding the important pass. Indeed, information from a party of Americans encountered on the road clearly indicated that they were *not*, but that the enemy probably were, as there was a road block ! As the Commanding Officer later remarked, ' the situation was obscure and bore some resemblance to that which prevailed in France in June 1940.' Investigation of the road northwards showed that it was blocked by American transport, and there was no sign of the Battalion's fighting vehicles coming down it. In these disheartening circumstances Neilson adopted the bold course. He took his one remaining company forward down the road, and finding no enemy at all he put them into position guarding the pass. Moving back up the road again he found his American superior officer who had received such alarming information about enemy numbers on the east side of the river that he had decided that the withdrawal must follow another axis on the west bank. This meant yet one more complete turn-round of everybody and everything. ' C ' Company was retrieved from the pass and turned about ; and just as Neilson was wondering how he would ever get these orders through to the missing two companies, he found Major Wilson on the road reporting that they were all down off the mountain, their direct route having been blocked by a precipice.[1] Wilson's comments and those of his men on being told to retrace their steps are fortunately not available. It must have been about 1 a.m. that the Battalion marched off again westwards, in deep snow, down the track they had so lately traversed. It was 5.30 before they reached the ford south of Unsan-Ni, and 9.30 by the time the transport had dropped them in the harbour area where ' B ' Echelon had safely arrived. This remarkable excursion into the mountains was christened ' The Cavalry Canter,' by the Jocks, and was never forgotten. They had marched and countermarched on two water-bottles in thirty-six hours, climbed and descended colossal heights, and driven their ancient vehicles in circles, all in the filthiest weather conditions. Yet at no time was the enemy encountered (though there was tangible evidence that he was no more than an hour away), and so nothing was apparently achieved. It was certainly one of the more extraordinary interludes of the war ; and although when looking back on it some funnier aspects became discernible, this was not until a long, long time afterwards.

This time the Brigade was to make a really big bound

---

[1] Credit for this amazing cross-country march goes to Lieutenant R. Wilson of the Highland Light Infantry, attached to ' B ' Company.

of about 120 miles to the south, although this (like the
instructor's lesson) was to be broken up into 'easy stages.'
There was no telling what this might mean. It was clear
that the Allied offensive had failed and the front was
crumbling under this entirely fresh Chinese offensive, but
the extent of the penetration was not by any means easy to
calculate. It seemed probable at the time that too much
reliance had been placed in the R.O.K. (South Korean)
divisions, for the first news of a break-through was on their
front ; but if the Corps reserve was withdrawing 120 miles,
the next front line appeared problematical. True, there was
no panic rush about the rearward movement, at least as
far as the Commonwealth Brigade was concerned. At
every stage of their journey they occupied a defensive
position, and dug themselves in, for none could say with
accuracy from which direction or in what strength the
enemy might appear. Providentially the other side made
no attempt to intervene in the air, so there was one less
problem to worry about. And thus, in their borrowed
transport, and followed by their own creaky old fighting
vehicles, the Battalion journeyed southwards again. Occa-
sionally they marched (once they did twelve miles to the
pipes before the ferrying vehicles were able to lift them) but
usually they motored, following the 'Nottingham' signs.[1]
Yul-Li, Singye, Sibyon-Ni (where they spent four days)
gradually faded astern, until on 11th December, they
reached Uijongbu which, little though they guessed it,
was to be their 'Shanty Town' home for Christmas and
Hogmanay. As may well be imagined, this long march in
winter by way of indifferent Korean roads played havoc
with the Battalion's transport. They developed ghastly
mechanical defects, they refused to start ; in fact, they
almost broke the spirit of their own indomitable drivers.
Some of them even had to be destroyed and left behind,
though these were very few indeed. But there is no doubt

[1] All units of 27 Brigade were allotted a code name beginning with N.
(See Battalion Christmas Card, Plate 16.)

that the machines were very nearly worn out, for even the usually taciturn *War Diary* notes :

> ' It is appropriate to record at this stage that our transport was in very poor shape. It had already done many miles in Hong Kong, and had only had a superficial overhaul before coming to Korea where it had been worked hard with very little time for maintenance.'

And in saying that much the author said a mouthful ! The fact was that the state of their fighting vehicles had reduced the Battalion to a static role, which is not to be wondered at when the carriers were obliged to leave early in the morning with the harbour party in the faint hope that this decent start would enable them to reach their destination not too long after the Battalion in its borrowed lorries ! This being so, it was perhaps fortunate that the Battalion was selected for the duty of protecting IX Corps H.Q. and became known as the ' Palace Guard.' As usual this involved a sudden change of plan, for they had reached Singye late at night on 6th December, and were just occupying their defensive position next morning when the orders came to move to Sibyon-Ni eighteen miles away for this duty. Away went Major Sloane with the harbour party, and away went the Colonel and the company commanders to get their jobs done before the rest of the Battalion arrived. As it was, the men only reached the place one hour before dark, and had barely time to site their weapon slits and start digging. This time they stayed four days before going on to ' Journey's End,' which meant an early rise at 04.00 hours on 11th December and a journey of 102 miles.

In all these moves, a great deal of responsibility rested on Sloane, the second-in-command, and his harbour party. They constituted what was in former days called an ' advanced party ' or a ' billeting party,' and their job was to find a suitable place for the Battalion to stretch itself in the new area. Both tactical and administrative aspects had to be considered in making his choice, and Sloane can never have had an easy task in consequence. Of course, by this time a standing drill had been laid down for the operations of the harbour party, and as its composition was usually the same on all occasions its efficiency grew accordingly. But no two moves were ever alike, and there were frequently some totally unforseen problems to be solved. Certainly Sibyon-Ni and the local protection of Corps H.Q. there gave the second-in-command an unusually heavy headache, as he found so many bodies of troops in the area that he experienced the utmost difficulty in securing any room for the Battalion to carry out its task. But he succeeded—indeed he never failed in this respect. There is no doubt that tact and patience are essential military virtues. Hopes were high that the Battalion might be concentrated at last in this rather indifferent film-set called ' Weejongboo.' They were short-lived, for ' B ' Company was almost at once sent off to guard the ' advanced portion ' of IX Corps H.Q. which was retreating still farther south of Seoul to a place called Ichon. They moved ; but not before joining in the general rejoicing at Neilson's D.S.O. ' for action on the Naktong,' news of which had just come through. When the Colonel gets that decoration the whole of his Battalion gains a foot in stature, as it were. They realise that they have ' put up a good show ' under his leadership, and their pride is immense. It is justifiable pride in a job well done ; and, vicariously, they claim the honour for their own. And so this just award was celebrated in sincere but sober fashion, and everyone was delighted and proud at this fresh honour heaped upon the Regimental name.

It was round about this time that an unknown but sympathetic American unit called ' Charlie ' Company, 3rd Chemical Mortar Battalion, came under command of the Argylls. The Battery Commander was, appropriately enough for two obvious reasons, called Charlie Snow, and it did not take him long to associate himself body and soul with the Jocks. He soon wore a Regimental badge pinned to his breast, and his short stout figure weighing (as he would put it) 200 pounds rapidly became a familiar feature of the Battalion area. (He later admitted to the loss of three stone after serving three months with the Argylls, though this may have been modesty on his part.) On his own estimation (which proved correct) he was the best poker player in the American Army, and it was against his principles to ' raise on three of a kind.' He never did it— ' No, Sir.' With him he brought the greatest of forward observation officers, ' Lootenant' Tom Holcomb from Pistol Ridge, Mississippi, ' where the biggest catfish are found ; Tom Kolbes, Dale Henry and Bill King, all first-class fellows. They shared the fortunes of the Battalion until it embarked some four months later, and it is safe to say that they and their unit were not officially, but affectionately, attached to the Argyll and Sutherland Highlanders.

During these days it became known that a ' Korean Presidential Citation ' had been awarded to the Commonwealth Brigade for its defence of the Naktong River line and its advance thereafter. There was naturally some curiosity about it, and it was eventually made clear that the distinction was not exactly a medal, although it meant that an extremely gay ribbon might be worn on the battle-dress sleeve—if permission were given. It has not yet been given. The citation was to have been presented to representatives of units in the Brigade by General Walton H. Walker, the American Army Commander, and it was while the parade was formed up awaiting his arrival that the news came of his death in a motor accident. The presentation was therefore made by General Milburn, though his successor in Command was later announced to be General Matthew B. Ridgeway.

All thoughts now turned towards the approaching Christmas, and everyone tried to brighten up their not unduly cheerful surroundings. True, it was not customary to celebrate this peculiarly Christian feast in a Presbyterian community that recked of nothing but the old pagan Hogmanay. Yet the Colonel decided he would follow the ancient Latin saying ' *Carpe Diem*,' for he could not tell where the Battalion might find itself as the New Year dawned. So all the necessary preparations as for New Year's Day were made, and eventually carried out. The shacks and bivouacs were decorated with whatever could be found ; and the cooks, mindful of Thanksgiving Day, set about thawing the turkeys. And on the 25th December the traditional New Year's Day routine was observed in a snowstorm, when the Commanding Officer, musically preceded by the Pipe-Major and accompanied by his Adjutant and Second-in-Command, visited all companies as they ate their Christmas dinner. It was a good one—here is the Menu. But even as the customary greetings were being

---

New Year's Day

MENU

Tomato Juice Cocktail
Relish Tray

ROAST TURKEY

Celery Dressing   Giblet Gravy
Cranberry Sauce

Snowflake Potatoes   Candied Sweet Potatoes
Whole Kernel Corn   Garden Green Peas
Bread and Butter

Fruit Cake   Mincemeat Pie
Coffee

Assorted Nuts   Hard Candies
Fresh Fruit

Plate 18   Lieutenant-Colonel G. L. Neilson D.S.O.

Plate 22. Pipe and Side Drums, and Colour party of the 51st Highland Division.

exchanged the peaceful pattern of life was being changed, and by nightfall the information came that Corps H.Q. was moving to Seoul next morning. The usual 'move machinery' was set in motion on 26th, only to be stopped, to everybody's inconvenience, before midday. Thus the Battalion found itself still in the same place for Hogmanay, and reckoned itself safe for the double event. A football mysteriously appeared, and the sergeants traditionally challenged the officers to a football match on New Year's Day in these terms :

CHALLENGE TO MORTAL COMBAT

We, the undersigned, of this Most Illustrious Regiment, to wit the Argyll and Sutherland High-landers, hereby, with malice aforethought, challenge our officers to meet and engage us in Battle at the Ignoble, unroyal and Prehistoric game of Ball of Foote, on the morning of 1st January 1951, at 10.00 hrs : the said game to be contested under Articles 324 of the Bulgarian Koran, viz : no holds barred and artificial dentures carried behind the left clavicle. All eyes, accidently or otherwise, removed, to be handed into the Bn. Orderly Room for safe custody. Remains littering the arena to be respectfully trans-ported to some Christian place of interment in the interests of humanity and the San Miguel Brewery Ltd.

An unusual feature in the customary routine was that Major Wilson, Pipe-Major McGlinn and some others went into Seoul and recorded a broadcast for the Scottish Programme at home. Finally, the Sergeants' Mess held what the *War Diary* discreetly describes as ' a small party to which the sergeants of the Middlesex and the Australians were welcomed as were the officers of the Battalion.' It took its traditional course—even to 'Auld Lang Syne'—but 'the sound of revelry by night' was interrupted (as on a former historic occasion) by gunfire, and the subsequent activities bore hardly on those whose enthusiasm for 1951 had been extreme. The orders to move north and cover the withdrawal of everybody through Seoul came at 6.30 a.m. on 1st January ; at 8.30 the Commanding Officer went forward, and at 10 o'clock the Battalion followed. This time it appeared that it was a case of ' what we're going on with this morning is rearguards.' The operation took four days, although (oddly enough) it involved no contact with the enemy. Apart from the inevitable change of plan, the operation boiled down to the Brigade holding the two bridges —the main bridge over the Han River and ' C ' Company with the Americans on the ' Al Jolson '—for forty-eight hours while the I Corps, IX Corps and 29th British Brigade (the other rearguard) crossed them. Luckily a company commander recorded his impressions of this episode (for it was no more) and he described the last night in Seoul in these words :

> ' Seoul is a town with an atmosphere—unlike Pusan and Taegu which are merely towns with smells. It is very large and straggling and quite high hills rise in the middle ! Try and imagine a city completely empty—the trams and buses still, the houses deserted, here and there a fire burning, the mutter of gunfire to the north, and a steady stream of homeless plodding their weary way south—and you have some idea of the atmosphere. . . . It was an eerie feeling driving through the empty streets, visiting the posts in a dying city.'

One curious thing about this critical withdrawal is that it was effected without any interference on the part of the enemy, and the Battalion was enabled to retire with dignity across its bridges without firing a shot—claiming to be the last of the Army—as did the 2nd Battalion across the Causeway at Singapore some nine years before. Another oddity is that the Battalion set off on its task less 'B' Company which was still at Ichon with Corps H.Q.; but that during the operation it was not only joined by this company but also by the newly resurrected 'D' Company which had been forming under Captain Howat at the same place. The final withdrawal from Seoul was a nightmare of road movement on every sort of conveyance and complicated by refugees and traffic jams. It began at 07.00 hours on 4th January and finished at 05.00 hours the next day. It was seventeen miles to Suwon, the first stage, and that took six hours; so the rate of progress can be gauged. Destination was a place called Yodonae and signified the low-water mark of the Allied retreat, for the next day they were sent forward again some thirty miles to Changhowon-Ni (alias Frostbite Ridge) which was to be their station for the next month. So ended an undistinguished withdrawal— except that it was observed that the last man out of Seoul, in his siren-screeching jeep, was General Ridgeway. It was taken as an omen.

For the first time since they left Hong Kong the Battalion was now concentrated and formed into a Headquarter company and four Rifle companies. This was a gradual return to their original organisation before they mobilised, and was another step towards making them better balanced as a fighting unit. It was generally welcomed among the men, because 'D' Company was formed of those who had formerly belonged to it and had never, in spirit, severed their allegiance. *Esprit de compagnie* is seldom saluted in military writing, but it has a great bearing on *esprit de corps*. Regardless of company, all are determined to uphold and increase the reputation of the Battalion; but when this corporate result has been achieved, every properly commanded company convinces itself that it has played the major part in producing this satisfactory state of affairs. And so it follows that the more companies there are, the stronger is the collective morale of the unit, for it is well known that no self-respecting company can be anything less than ' the best in the whole (censored) battalion.'

It was at this point that ' B ' Company were able to shoot their line about being ' Household Troops ' at Ichon with the rearmost portion of Corps H.Q. Their tales were indeed remarkable. It appeared that, to units as remote and inaccessible as ' Rear Corps H.Q.,' these ' combat troops ' of a foreign nation were something of a proprietary curiosity like creatures from another world. Visitors were conducted reverently round their defensive (combat) positions, and the Jocks' tales of the distant front line were listened to with considerable respect. Their ' combat souvenirs ' of all sorts and sizes had a high commercial value ; and even the G.1098 Machete, artistically part-worn so as to fall into this category, was known to change hands for an astronomical sum. Those were the days, and they were heroes then. They were royally entertained on Christmas Day, but retribution fell the next day on the revellers who had exceeded the bounds of good order and military discipline. Though the Company office was represented by an upturned box in the snow, behind it, on another, sat Captain Colin Mitchell ; and with the aid of Sergeant-Major Murray, justice was done in the customary British way. It didn't matter if it was Colchester, Kowloon or Korea, the same old routine held good :

> Escort and accused—'SHUN
> Hat off (Hat—of some sort—is thrown
> down on snow)
> Right TURN
> Quick MARCH—LEFRILEFRILEFRIHALT
> Left TURN
> Private McClucherty—SIR (introduction)

Justice was then administered, followed by the usual noisy, brisk and undignified exit. It impressed the Allies greatly. It even moved one of them to observe to C.S.M.

Murray with respectful admiration : ' Gee, this is a rugged outfit. It beats West Point.' Though slightly ignorant of its exact significance, ' B ' Company accepted this tribute in the spirit in which it was meant. Altogether it was reckoned to have been an unusual, though commercially sound, detachment ; and of course it improved enormously in retrospect and anecdote.

Changhowon-Ni, which was originally intended as a temporary position, became rather more permanent than anyone had foreseen, and in fact the Battalion spent a month there. However, it was clear that a further move south was still contemplated, and reconnaissances of positions in that direction were made as a matter of course. But it never came to that, and there was no action beyond patrolling to gain contact with a strangely inactive enemy. It was generally thought that the enemy's inaction must have been due to his disliking the winter as much as the Jocks did. They found it quite phenomenally cold, and when one night the temperature dropped to twenty degrees below zero they could find no words suitable to describe it. Everything froze in a few minutes. Hot water poured into a car radiator was ice before it reached the bottom ; and even ' Anti-Freeze ' in a solution of one to one was not proof against this sort of weather.

Sometimes, by way of variation, there was a thaw which caused almost equal misery on account of the ghastly mud and the treacherous road conditions, but more usually the biting cold Manchurian wind scourged them and covered them in snow. Yet, even though they were well equipped by now with proper winter uniforms and warm woollen things from home, they shivered as the cold penetrated to the marrow of their bones, and prayed the locals were speaking the truth in saying the warm weather began in February. Inevitably cases of frost-bite occurred, for normal methods of warming the extremities of the body and drying wet socks twice a day could not be adopted in the line. However, in case the frost-bite menace assumed serious proportions in this indescribable winter, the Colonel gave permission to relax certain operational restrictions. As a result, small fires, carefully screened for smoke, were allowed to be lit in recesses dug into the side of the trenches. These proved invaluable as a means of warming up men before turning in, and of drying their wet socks. They certainly checked the incidence of frost-bite, and the Battalion had easily the lowest number of cases of any front-line Allied unit in Korea.

In the absence of hostile action, boredom became the soldier's main enemy. Day after day the *War Diary* reports ' Another quiet day,' ' An uneventful day,' ' Patrols had nothing to report.' Yet it is also able to record one or two interesting events. There was, for instance, the news that Kenny Muir had been posthumously awarded the Victoria Cross for his courageous leadership on Hill 282 in September. This lit a quiet fire of pride throughout the frost-bound Battalion, for all knew that this was the only fitting reward for such gallantry as his. There was comforting warmth, too, in the knowledge that this had been recognised by His Majesty.

Then again, it tells of the return of the first leave party from Japan with tales of the fleshpots that roused their numbed compatriots to enviously derisive observations. This leave system was certainly one of the blessings of life, for it acted as a tonic for tired men, and gave a tangible hope of seven days in civilisation far from the degrading discomfort of their present circumstances. Though it was calculated that the odds against your name coming out of the hat were 33 to 1, nevertheless there was always that odd chance for which you could live and hope and plan. Turning from welfare to warfare with an unsettling swerve, that same impartial chronicle reveals that on 22nd January the 16th Field Regiment of the Royal New Zealand Artillery joined the Commonwealth Brigade as its own private artillery support, a necessity for which (as we know) they had waited overlong. (What the *Diary* does *not* record is the opening demonstration of close support by 162 Battery which planted a salvo of well-meant shells in No. 6 Platoon's area and 'warmed them up more than somewhat' as the Thin Red Line later remarked !)

It is in static periods such as this that men learn to make their own amusements and devise means of staving off inertia. So they followed the football fortunes in the home papers and magazines now reaching them, played 'Housey-Housey' and other stranger games they learned from their Allies, and generally groused about their first-class free issues from the 'PX.' This remarkable institution would send you a weekly 'buckshee' issue of chocolate, soap, razor blades and kindred things which the British soldier would normally have bought for hard cash from his NAAFI shop, had there been such a thing. It was really the razor blades that caused most of the complaints. Being intended for American troops they were predominantly of the single-edge type, and therefore did not fit the standard British safety razor, for which comparatively few double-edged blades were obtainable. Though this caused some despondency among the men, who quite rightly wished to appear properly shaved in spite of the Chinese and the Korean winter, it caused much merriment among American pressmen who regarded this and the British love of tea as two of the funniest jokes of the war and worked them threadbare.

Of course it seemed quite natural for footballs to appear in a front-line position, though nobody could ever quite account for their appearance. And though organised games were out of the question at this period, gangs of men could usually be seen behind the line kicking a ball about on any sort of flat and frozen surface. 'A' and 'C' Companies, with more originality, organised a shooting match with all forms of small arms against their old friends of the 5th Regimental Combat Team. Admittedly it was only a matter of tin cans set up in a paddy field ; but Scotland won the match. The Americans, however, carried off (and cherished ever after) the booby prize which was a Korean chamber pot (splashless type), tastefully decorated with blue and white flowers in honour of the United Nations. But the New Zealand sportsman who drew his revolver and knocked his target flat with one shot at fifty yards was, literally, the hit of the piece. As for mental recreation, there was always the American Forces Network from Tokyo which you could get on your 'welfare radio' and which would provide hours of jive, jitterbug and swing sentimentality. There must be many who are still getting into trouble for singing 'Irene' at inappropriate moments! But naturally their own music was heard also. Though the pipers all had a soldier's duty to do in the field, each individual practised on his own when opportunity occurred. In each company the piper was employed at his headquarters, mainly as a runner. Pipe-Major McGlinn became the self-constituted personal escort to the Commanding Officer from the very early days and accompanied him everywhere. And, of course, both he and Sergeant Robertson perpetuated the campaign with two tunes named in honour of Colonel Neilson and Major Muir.

Inaction also regularly produces one other effect, and that is rumours. 'Frostbite Ridge' was no exception to this fine old rule, and the rumours covered every sort of likely and unlikely contingency. Since most of them had a purely local significance they are hardly worth repetition here; but one of another kind seems worthy of a wider public. It was January 1951, and the Jocks were saying that the 'Scottish Nationalists would return the Stone of Destiny if the Argylls were returned to Stirling!'

As this dreary month drew to its appointed end it became clear that some activity was being planned, and sure enough, on the 25th, elements of 1st U.S. Cavalry Division were advancing through the Battalion area for a 'limited offensive.' 'Frostbite Ridge' faded out of the map as a front-line, and the Argylls were once more in Corps Reserve and at two hours' notice to move anywhere.

The orders came on 4th February, and they moved to
Yoju, a few miles north of them, where in spite of constant
patrolling in strength for a week they could make no contact
with the enemy. Yet the information was that the enemy
were about to attack in strength, so defensive plans were
laid and the whole Brigade dug itself in and prepared to
meet the threat. But it never materialised ; the plans were
' all changed ' (presumably those of the Chinese also) and
on 13th February there began a painstaking and mountainous
advance which was to last a month. As far as the Battalion
was concerned, it was the penultimate round of their war,
though none knew it at that time. It was one of the many
occasions on which the tide had temporarily turned, and
once more the operation orders were concerned with
objectives and not with defensive positions. The general
direction was still northwards, and the tendency of all
hearts was upwards. ' If winter comes, can spring be far
behind ? ' The locals now said the snow would definitely
vanish in March, and though the Jocks did not entirely
believe them, they took some comfort from their apparently
unfounded optimism.

Chapter V

THE LAST ROUND

Now began the epoch that was known as ' Chink chasing.' It was a determined attempt to shift the enemy (no longer just ' Gooks ') from their mountain positions, and show that the Allies could beat them on foot as well as in their vehicles. In this offensive was seen the new spirit of the 8th Army inculcated by General Ridgeway, whose insistence on forward and not rearward movement was by now manifesting itself. But it was no ' Victory March,' this process of dislodging the Chinese Communists from their well-prepared and camouflaged mountain positions. It was a slow business, and one with which the Commonwealth Brigade had long been familiar—that of turning the enemy off the top of his mountain and at the same time securing yourself with a ' foot on the ground.' This technique, so it appeared, had now been adopted by the whole of the 8th Army. ' Barrelling down the road ' was off—at any rate, for the moment. It was simply the old tactical story of making sure of one position before attacking the next ; and so company passed through company, and battalion through battalion in succession for a period of four weeks. Fortunately the Brigade was now ' square ' for the first time, as the 2nd Battalion of Princess Patricia's Canadian Light Infantry had now joined, and so the tactical formation of ' two up and two back ' could be adopted. The ' Commonwealth ' unity also was broadened and strengthened, and laid the foundation of the Commonwealth Division that was later to be formed.

It must be confessed at once that the Argylls played a serviceable but unspectacular part in this month of progress. Seldom were they in contact, and seldom did they encounter opposition and incur casualties. Nor were they ever involved in any major action. It was just steady plodding ahead in acute discomfort with apparently nothing much to show at the end of the day. Throughout it all they were supported ably and effectively by 162 Battery of the Royal New Zealand Artillery under Major Dinty Moore and by Charlie Snow's famous mortars. And perhaps this is the place to record, without gilding the lily, that the co-operation of these two units was not of the sort that is confined by Operation Orders. It was the ' English-speaking Union ' at its best—though the guarded and non-committal phrases of the *War Diary* do not venture to say so.

In an earlier war the expression ' spring offensive ' was a common term. In this one, it was suddenly quite notice-able that spring and the offensive had coincided. Writing home on 11th February—the day the Argylls were raised—an officer said, ' It has been a lovely day with a very strong sun which it was a pleasure to sit in—thawing hard all the time with a temperature equivalent to a May afternoon.' Spring, in fact, was definitely in the air, and the locals who had prophesied warm weather in March did not, after all, appear such extreme optimists. That is not to say that the spring which follows a deadly winter does so with a light step. It has its drawbacks, as, for instance, when they suddenly had a foot of snow in the first week of March, and when the thaw conditions of 22nd February produced, not a day of golden sunshine, but one of unremitting rain.

' It had been most unpleasant during the day with rain, and the companies were soaked to the skin. After a very wet and uncomfortable night the Rifle Companies managed to dry out, and rations were carried up to them by Korean porters.'—*War Diary*

These Korean porters became an essential part of the Battalion organisation in this phase of the campaign. It is not too much to say that the supply problem could not have been solved without their assistance, for you cannot imagine men climbing to 3,000 feet, digging in, and then having to fetch up their own supplies and keep off the enemy simultaneously. These porters were really wonderful and carried the most fantastic loads on their ' A ' frames (see the illustration on Plate 6). Curiously enough, they became (literally) very attached to their companies, and were often to be found ' brewing up ' with a section of Jocks in the greatest of *camaraderie*.

The month's operations came to an end on 13th March with ' A ' Company occupying the record height of 752 metres—approximately 2,500 feet. The orders went out, and down, with the agility of mountain goats, came the hardy hairy Highlanders to the Brigade rest area in a dry river bed surrounded by paddy-fields. It was not in any way a ' namely sort of place ' ; but at least it was out of sight and sound of the enemy. For the second time in six months they took off their boots and had a hot shower. There was new clothing and equipment and (not so good) F.F.I. inoculations. It was also the first time that the Battalion had been concentrated for six months. Possibly this seems a small consideration to some people, but when you have been moving for a long time through a strange and utterly unattractive country in isolated Company groups, you begin to long for a corporate existence again. This is the ordinary manifestation of Regimental spirit. And when this aspiration can be met the result is the most pronounced upward curve in the ' morale graph ' that you ever saw.

In this instance the Commanding Officer took the earliest opportunity to turn out the pipes and drums in the kilt on 15th March to play ' Retreat.' There is no better method of brisking up tired troops than this, and the result was exactly what had been intended. They led the Brigade past the Brigadier after he had presented American decorations, and cheered the hearts of the exiled Scots, not all of whom were serving in the ranks of the Regiment !

This was the first possibility of organised games and the chance was of course seized with both hands—' in that manner

there' (as the instructor always says).   Apparently the
transformation of the unpromising dry river bed into a
competent sports ground was a communal effort which
looked like a miracle to some of the very young soldiers, who
did not know the Regular Army's addiction to this sort of
thing.   One of them naïvely wrote :

> ' It looked absolutely hopeless when we arrived ; but
> next day it was a different place altogether.   There were
> football pitches, a Rugby pitch and a basket ball pitch—
> all the boys had mucked in and got things organised.
> There were games on every minute of the day.'

The Battalion at any rate maintained the Regimental
football tradition and beat all comers—a surprisingly
satisfactory result when all the circumstances are considered.
But though this might be described as a ' set-piece gladiatorial
show,' the most popular event of that memorable ten days
was the ' potted sports.'   The New Zealanders emerged as
the victors of this contest—amongst other assets, their Maori
tug-of-war team was quite invincible.

Those invaluable ten days of rest and recreation passed
only too quickly, but they had played their intended part
in heartening up the soldiers for their next round.   As far
as the Jocks were concerned it was to be their last.   Sadly
enough, the end of this period of resting was also the end
of the Brigadier's active service in Korea.   He left for
Hong Kong and was later promoted Major-General and
given command of the 2nd Division in Germany.   To those
who had served under him in this arduous campaign it
seemed a fitting reward for his six months' distinguished
command of the British Commonwealth token force.   Though
this is the story of the Argylls, it is the story of their cam-
paigning under Coad's command and, therefore, it cannot
be completed without a personal reference to him.   To his
officers and men it must have appeared the luckiest thing in
the war that he was selected to lead them.   His ability to
establish friendly relations with the superior American

commanders ensured the most considerate treatment for his Brigade ; and the important tasks assigned to him from time to time indicate the reliability and respect which it was universally accorded. As for his subordinates, they had complete confidence in his judgment, and every man felt that if he had made the plan (whether welfare or warfare) then it was a good one. He made a great reputation for himself among our Allies and our Dominions. And in the ranks of the Argylls there was widespread and genuine regret at his departure as for that of a close friend who had shared their dangers and discomforts as well as their triumphs, and had given them the chance to write a new page of Regimental history. His place at the helm was taken by Brigadier Burke who steered them through the final phase of their operations.

Not that the next three weeks' operations differed in any way from those that they had preceded. It was still mountain warfare—only in a different area, near Kapyong, thirty-five miles north-west; and the mountains were 'kind of high '—up to 4,000 feet. It was the old familiar game of moving in transport along the only motorable road in the valley ; and making good the hills on either side of it. The quality of the Chinese Communist had been accurately assessed by now, of course, and it was realised that he was a tenacious and tough fighter of similar class to the Japanese, possessed of considerable skill in handling machine guns and mortars. He could be expected to remain in his hill positions until prodded out with a bayonet, and it was usual for him to do so. He was, in fact, a first-class soldier, with whom you could take no chances.

On 4th April the Argylls ran into their first (and last) trouble in these mountains. It was not a day of heavy fighting ; simply the routine business of attacking the next ridge ahead of the one which had already been secured. ' A ' and ' D ' Companies were attacking, and there appeared to be a few Chinese and some machine guns on the objective. But they took their toll of the Jocks, as the list of casualties showed. These included two of the platoon commanders, Lieutenants Cawthorne and Milner, who were both killed. Milner was a Regular officer of the Dorsetshire Regiment who had volunteered for Korea and only recently arrived. The former had served with 'A' Company throughout the campaign, and it was a tragedy that he should have been taken just as the Battalion's task was ending. The objective had not been captured by nightfall, but was successfully secured next day with the aid of medium artillery support. That was the day (5th April) that 'B' Company had some casualties in a minefield (an unexpected hazard) ; and 'C' Company, 3,000 feet high up on Daffodil, found themselves established exactly on the renowned 38th Parallel. There was nothing to mark it this time ; but when the Brigade had crossed it in the retreat from Pyongyang there had been a large notice board erected by the Americans which read, 'You are now crossing the 38th Parallel by kind permission of the Chinese 4th Army.'

By 8th April the Jocks had attacked their last hill and soon after the Battalion was withdrawn into the valley at Karim as Brigade reserve ; and it was during the ten days in which they were there that the news came of their relief. No date and no unit was mentioned, so as to avoid any repetition of the memorable November disappointment, but all were given to understand that it was imminent. Hopes went soaring skywards with this wonderful news ; and what might have been fiction became almost fact when on the 18th the Brigade began to be relieved by 19th R.O.K. Regiment and went back to Kapyong. It seemed too good to be true—and it was. They were not off yet; they were not under the starter's orders and the flag had not yet fallen. Nevertheless all the routine signs could only mean that 'the big boat with the tartan funnels' was already lined up for them.

On 19th a small advance party left for Hong Kong ; and on the next night the officers gave a farewell party whose chief feature was a locally distilled form of Atholl

Brose. It may have been coincidence, of course, but on the following day the Battalion was declared 'non-operational' on account of its impending move, so the way was left free for entertainment.

There was much handing over of windproof jackets, string vests and things peculiar to Korea, amongst the latter being 'Lulu.' This was a native pig that had been acquired in its infancy by Sergeant Ball, the cook sergeant, some time in the Naktong River period. It had grown during its time on the strength of the Battalion from an attractive juvenile to a monstrous matron, and in doing so had successfully survived all the hazards of war. It was finally turned over to the head Korean porter attached to the Argylls who had expressed a desire to breed from her. He received the best wishes of all bacon-loving soldiers for this enterprising idea.

On Sunday, 22nd April there was a Brigade church parade for all Battalions—the last of its kind. That same evening 162 New Zealand Field Battery entertained a large party from the Battalion with a 'Haka' and feast in the Maori style. The *plat du jour* was a whole bullock cooked on red-hot stones in a hollow in the ground. This was covered over and water was then poured into it through a small hole in the top. The effect of the steam rising from the heated stones produced the most delicious dish which was one of the gastronomic memories of the war. And, after the meal, the New Zealanders gave traditional songs and war dances until it was time to go home. It was the last really enjoyable night they spent in Korea. By dawn the next day the situation on the Brigade sector was anything but firm ! The Chinese offensive had started the same night, but rather too well, and had scored an alarming initial success along the general line of the 6th R.O.K. Division in front. This must have appeared to the Jocks like the hand of fate again intervening at the very last moment to snatch away their long-cherished hope just as it was on the point of being fulfilled. One can well imagine their feelings, though they are not exactly expressed in this

Plate 20   Brigadier Coad (with Lieutenant-Colonel Neilson)

contemporary account which appeared in the Regimental magazine :

'On Monday 23rd we woke to the sound of gunfire and noticed several disquieting signs. Firstly, the Middlesex had not run up their Union Jack and Regimental flag outside their camp ; and, secondly, there was a certain ominous activity round Battalion Headquarters, and the sight of company commanders hurrying to and fro boded ill. Sure enough, by midday, the Colonel and his minions were seen striding over the neighbouring hills, the wireless sets and tools that we had packed away were reissued, and, with the rest of 27th Brigade, we took to the hills and prepared our positions. We knew then that the Chinese had attacked in force, and that all the ground that we had won in the last fortnight had been lost in twenty-four hours.

'We dug in and waited, while through the night the noise of battle approached. By dawn the sound of small arms and mortar fire could be heard in the Australian sector, but apart from the all too familiar stream of refugees no-one had come near us.'

The Battalion was due to move to Inchon for embarkation on 24th. Of course the Americans had, not unnaturally, asked for them to be retained as the Brigade front was one of those affected ; but the original orders stood, and the Argylls were in their vehicles and away by 11 a.m. And only just in time, for the Colonel was at Brigade H.Q. when a second message arrived to say they were to stay ! However, material resources (or lack of them) solved the problem. There were not sufficient vehicles and special technical equipment to be of use to both the Argylls and their relief (The King's Own Scottish Borderers, already on their road up to the front), and so the Brigadier decided against any change of plan. Meanwhile the Battalion, blissfully ignorant of the fate they had so narrowly escaped, bowled along westwards and enjoyed the most pleasant drive they had ever done in Korea—along the only tarmac road it possesses. Their same correspondent wrote :

'It was a lovely afternoon, the road was clear of traffic, the hillsides were alive with a purple flower that made them seem covered with heather, and there was little dust. Indeed, at times, the only signs of war were the direction signs that we knew so well—Danger FWD, Swing, Lobster, Domino Red, Triple Nickel, Sandbag and, of course, the one that we were following this time—Keen.

'Seoul itself was very quiet, but looking even more derelict than ever, with the same Korean police standing on pedestals in the middle of each road intersection, blowing whistles madly at each and every vehicle as it passed. But when we were halfway through, an Australian Army signal jeep appeared—with siren screeching—in search of the Colonel. This, we were sure, was the recall ; but, no, it was only a signal from General Robertson wishing us " bon voyage," and we breathed again. On we went over the Han River by the same bridge that we had crossed in January—across the sandflats and on to the tarmac road that leads to Inchon. Surely, we thought, nothing could stop us now.'

On their road they had passed their old New Zealand companions in arms, still in action and supporting the Australians in the line ; and ten miles down the route at a road fork was seen, and saluted, the solitary figure of Charlie Snow—that strong Scottish supporter !

They met the K.O.S.B. on the road. Little was said, but Colonel Neilson indicated to Colonel Macdonald that the battle was on and the visitors were just in time for it. Many Argylls were left behind to serve with the incoming Battalion, just as the Borderers had sent their men with the first Scottish Battalion in the field. Their individual fortunes are partially shown in the appendices to this book ; but the deeds of the Borderers have already become history.

The soldiers' reactions on leaving the front were various,

but they ranged from relief at getting clear to regret for the Commonwealth comrades they had left behind to face the music. This, as somebody with the necessary experience observed, was exactly comparable to the feelings of those of the Regiment who were lucky enough to escape from Singapore in 1942. There is nothing new about it.

Inchon was reached late in the afternoon, and after loading their ship they spent a dismally uncomfortable last night ashore in a Korean schoolhouse. Early the next morning it was ' Outside with your rifles ' for the last time in the war, and the Battalion was on its way to embark, cheered on their way by the pipers of the Royal Ulster Rifles recently arrived with the 29th Brigade. Their ship was to be the U.S.S. *Montrose*, curiously named for carrying a 'Campbell' Regiment, as David Wilson (himself a Graham) observed. This time it was a proper transport and no improvisation was necessary. So they relaxed, officers and men, in the well-organised comfort of the American Navy and enjoyed the ministrations of their American hosts.

Never were weary warriors better fed or kindlier treated after a campaign than were the Jocks by the ship's company of *Montrose*. They had hardly distinguished between the sharp and the blunt end of the ship before they were getting outside a gigantic breakfast ; and the diet of T-bone steaks, ice-cream and Coca-cola was gastronomically bewildering ! But they liked it !

They sailed in the afternoon, but the Colonel has since confessed that he was ' a bit apprehensive until the screw actually started turning.' And well might he be, for he had learned one campaign lesson at least. It was that you must never disregard the possibility of the threat which begins with the words, ' It's all changed now.' However, no such signal was received, the screw turned, and the finest view of Korea was enjoyed by all. As their transport steamed out of the harbour she passed H.M.S. *Belfast* wearing the flag of Rear-Admiral Scott-Moncrieff, with the whole of the ship's company mustered to salute the

Battalion with three cheers. The Marine Band played on the quarterdeck, and as it ceased, a solitary piper in the kilt was seen and heard standing on a gun turret and playing the two Regimental marches, ' The Campbells are Coming ' and ' Hieland Laddie.' It was Engineer Lieutenant Scrimgeour's farewell to his brother Scots. The significance of this was not lost on the Highlanders, and every eye followed his movements as he ended his music, turned aft and saluted the quarterdeck and disappeared from view.

They landed at Hong Kong on 28th April and received a great welcome. It was all very pleasing and they enjoyed it very much, but their minds were still moving through a maze of memories. They had travelled far through the unknown land of Korea since August. They had passed from the apple orchards of the south, along the dusty miscalled roads that led to Waegwan, Seoul, Sariwon 'and places north '; they had survived the bitter winds of Pakchon and Kunuri, endured the shanties in the snow at Uibongju and ' climbed the highest mountains ' around Yoju. More than that, they had earned the respect and friendship of all their Allies in arms, and had maintained and enhanced the name of Scotland and of their Regiment throughout the world. Behind them they left their comrades, marked by the Cross, where never an Argyll and Sutherland Highlander fought or fell before. And back to that hallowed ground at Taegu their thoughts were turning, mindful of those who once had shared their lot. In unsought fellowship together they had faced realities and found their strength. Only a distant historian will be able to say what they actually achieved in their brief campaign. Though the survivors could not have said so, they had acquitted themselves in the spirit of those 14th-century champions of Scottish liberty :

' So long as there shall be but one hundred of us remain alive we shall never submit ourselves to domination . . . For it is not glory, it is not riches, neither is it honour, but it is liberty alone that we fight and contend for, which no honest man will lose but with his life.'

EPILOGUE

THE motto of the 1st Battalion is ' *Ne obliviscaris* '—the motto of Clan Campbell taken from their first Colonel. Though literally a negative injunction not to forget, it can equally well be interpreted as a positive command to remember ; and it was in this latter sense that the Battalion observed Sunday, 23rd September 1951, when they paraded at Hong Kong to commemorate their dead. It was appropriately the anniversary of the action at Hill 282, which had been their first major engagement in Korea ; and by a happy chance Captain Thring of H.M.S. *Ceylon* was able to be there and receive their salute on behalf of his ship.

The Rev. J. F. Macdonald, their chaplain through most of the campaign, conducted the brief and pointed service. Officers and men, dressed once again as Highlanders should be, listened as he said :

' Many years ago an old man called John had a vision of the kind of world the United Nations are trying to build—the ideal for which our comrades fought and died. This vision is something realisable in our day and generation, but it all starts with ourselves. We are the people who count—not the politicians. The first step to the rebuilding of a better world is the rebuilding of our lives.'

And, listening, they remembered : those who had sailed away with them a year ago, who had marched and climbed and fought and endured with them, and who had met their end in that Godless land. Had they died in vain for a vast ideal ?

' I saw a new heaven and a new earth.'

The wild insistent pipes and the marching feet defiantly made answer : ' There shall be no more death.'

APPENDIX A

Casualties from September 1950 to April 1951

*

KILLED IN ACTION

NAKTONG AREA

368568	Captain C. N. A. Buchanan	6 Sept. 50
19034531	Private T. Taylor	6 Sept. 50
22315311	Private T. Clarke (traffic accident at Taegu)	16 Sept. 50
14468918	Private A. Lorimer	18 Sept. 50
14185116	Private C. Howcroft (river crossing)	23 Sept. 50

HILL 282

50980	Major K. Muir	23 Sept. 50
407775	2nd Lieutenant M. D. W. Buchanan	23 Sept. 50
3608517	Private A. Holmes	23 Sept. 50
21127212	Private M. Dempsey	23 Sept. 50
14460095	Sergeant E. Pigg	23 Sept. 50
22186756	Private E. Hill	23 Sept. 50
2839717	Private A. McKelvie	23 Sept. 50
14475260	Private E. McLaughlin	23 Sept. 50
14467019	Private J. Cowan	23 Sept. 50
22272060	Private E. Barclay	23 Sept. 50
14490066	Corporal R. Whittington	23 Sept. 50
22316464	Private A. Annan	23 Sept. 50
22219896	Private W. Wood	23 Sept. 50

SOHUNG

14470871	Private R. Kinnie	23 Sept. 50

PYONGYANG

14190414	Private C. McHardy	22 Oct. 50

Pakchon

22247073	Private J. Foster	5 Nov. 50
22167158	Private G. Gordon	5 Nov. 50
19045827	Private R. Kemp	5 Nov. 50
19032209	Lance-Corporal R. Stark	5 Nov. 50
14483790	Sergeant N. Clark	5 Nov. 50
22176166	Private J. Livingston	5 Nov. 50

Karim

297324	Lieutenant J. A. C. Milner	4 April 51
407789	2nd Lieutenant M. J. D. Cawthorne	4 April 51

DIED OF WOUNDS

19033587	Private V. Coles	23 Sept. 50
19045332	Lance-Corporal D. Allan	22 Oct. 50
14450655	Corporal D. Paterson	4 Mar. 51

WOUNDED

Naktong Area

396085	Lieutenant G. Lloyd-Davies	5 Sept. 50
408459	2nd Lieutenant E. S. Hunter	5 Sept. 50
2979082	Sergeant T. Murray	5 Sept. 50
14461777	Sergeant A. Walker	6 Sept. 50
14189417	Private W. Sutherland	6 Sept. 50
14191015	Private D. Gilks	6 Sept. 50
21182607	Private D. Kelly	6 Sept. 50
14456953	Corporal J. Layton	6 Sept. 50
3188042	Private C. Bathgate	6 Sept. 50
22167179	Private J. Mutch	8 Sept. 50
22231771	Private W. Fyffe	8 Sept. 50
19033612	Private G. Grant	8 Sept. 50
19038591	Private J. Welsh	14 Sept. 50
22233699	Private P. Maguire	18 Sept. 50
21182161	Private G. Forrest	18 Sept. 50
14454176	Corporal C. Crout (river crossing)	21 Sept. 50
14462794	Private H. Clark (river crossing)	21 Sept. 50
22245121	Private J. Mutch (west of Taegu)	21 Sept. 50

HILL 282

397371	2nd Lieutenant J. R. R. Edington	23 Sept. 50
88487	Captain J. A. Penman M.C.	23 Sept. 50
397981	2nd Lieutenant P. M. K. Mackellar	23 Sept. 50
410797	2nd Lieutenant J. D. Stirling	23 Sept. 50
14467882	Private A. Proll	23 Sept. 50
14433324	Corporal N. McNaughton	23 Sept. 50
19034526	Private P. Quinn	23 Sept. 50
14477378	Lance-Corporal H. Ward	23 Sept. 50
14467523	Private A. Johanson	23 Sept. 50
19108105	Private P. Martin	23 Sept. 50
19031261	Corporal R. Sweeney	23 Sept. 50
22191635	Private J. Bell	23 Sept. 50
22164314	Private R. Hodgson	23 Sept. 50
22171626	Private D. Beardmore	23 Sept. 50
5437226	Sergeant J. O'Sullivan M.M.	23 Sept. 50
19040319	Lance-Corporal R. Syme	23 Sept. 50
22186881	Private W. Kelly	23 Sept. 50
22316483	Private R. Irving	23 Sept. 50
21128434	Private I. McKerrow	23 Sept. 50
22138875	Private A. Anderson	23 Sept. 50
19039823	Private R. Franks	23 Sept. 50
14471420	Lance-Corporal J. Fairhurst	23 Sept. 50
22256625	Sergeant J. Harrison	23 Sept. 50
14187413	Lance-Corporal R. Newton	23 Sept. 50
19037413	Lance-Corporal G. McEwan	23 Sept. 50
22167185	Private D. Simpson	23 Sept. 50
22273152	Private C. Campbell	23 Sept. 50
14198097	Private D. Male	23 Sept. 50
19042563	Private R. Vernon	23 Sept. 50
14758498	Private A. Roy	23 Sept. 50
22158886	Private A. Girvan	23 Sept. 50
19179456	Private J. Nelson	23 Sept. 50
14184550	Private R. Savage	23 Sept. 50
19037505	Private L. Bradshaw	23 Sept. 50
14463017	Private G. Davis	23 Sept. 50
21023452	Private D. Sidey	23 Sept. 50
22167183	Private I. Reid	23 Sept. 50
22176103	Private D. Frize	23 Sept. 50
22233299	Private R. Woodburn	23 Sept. 50
14456995	Private C. Hodkinson	23 Sept. 50
22176700	Private J. Esson	23 Sept. 50
21188219	Private J. Kennedy	23 Sept. 50
22203304	Lance-Corporal H. Saunders	23 Sept. 50

22186470	Private J. Poole	23 Sept. 50
22167173	Private A. Mackie	23 Sept. 50
22168143	Private D. Horsburgh	23 Sept. 50
21181560	Lance-Corporal H. Bird	23 Sept. 50
19048581	Private W. Pattison	23 Sept. 50
14189502	Corporal R. Vincent	23 Sept. 50
14191021	Private P. McGann	23 Sept. 50
22202780	Private J. Delaney	23 Sept. 50
22247152	Private J. Johnston	23 Sept. 50
14463874	Private A. Mitchell	23 Sept. 50
22256523	Private J. Anyon	23 Sept. 50
21126559	Private J. Smith	23 Sept. 50
14188719	Lance-Corporal D. Whitehouse	23 Sept. 50
14478861	Corporal D. Jenkins	23 Sept. 50
22176711	Private V. Kinnear	23 Sept. 50
14042622	Corporal M. Docherty	23 Sept. 50
22167161	Private C. Johnstone	23 Sept. 50
2986278	Sergeant W. Dunbar M.M.	23 Sept. 50
2979777	Private J. Hynds	23 Sept. 50
14464381	Lance-Corporal E. O'Kane	23 Sept. 50
22250542	Private McPherson	23 Sept. 50
22235957	Private A. McEntee	23 Sept. 50
21127998	Private R. McLaughlin	23 Sept. 50
2976114	Private A. Roger	23 Sept. 50
22316508	Private P. Sinclair	23 Sept. 50
14485729	Corporal W. McDonald	23 Sept. 50
22181514	Private W. Watts	23 Sept. 50
22314354	Private K. Davis	23 Sept. 50
22229895	Private S. Williamson	23 Sept. 50

SOHUNG

| 2976494 | Private J. O'Rourke | 17 Oct. 50 |

PYONGYANG

22162595	Private R. Dunaway	22 Oct. 50
21127061	Private I. Edgar	22 Oct. 50
21182815	Private M. Reid	22 Oct. 50
19043030	Private R. Millan	22 Oct. 50

Pakchon

58189	Major A. I. Gordon-Ingram	5 Nov. 50
14468637	Corporal J. Cree	5 Nov. 50
22523319	Private R. Gurr	5 Nov. 50
22186466	Private J. Meighan	5 Nov. 50
14450655	Corporal R. Paterson	5 Nov. 50
21128961	Lance-Corporal G. Robertson	5 Nov. 50
14161994	Private T. Lockhart	5 Nov. 50
88487	Major J. A. Penman m.c.	7 Nov. 50
411746	2nd Lieutenant E. S. Cunningham	7 Nov. 50
3128616	Corporal J. Campbell	7 Nov. 50
22167181	Private W. Nisbet	7 Nov. 50
14470976	Private L. Bolton	7 Nov. 50
3654469	Private P. Lythgoe	7 Nov. 50
22248891	Corporal K. Craig	7 Nov. 50
19038820	Corporal J. Thompson	8 Nov. 50
2930206	Private B. McDonald	8 Nov. 50
21128160	Private M. White	16 Nov. 50

Sunchon

22256468	Lance-Corporal K. Wallace	4 Dec. 50

Chonyon

411244	2nd Lieutenant A. J. Lauder	22 Feb. 51
14468637	Corporal J. Cree	13 Mar. 51
21181560	Lance-Corporal H. Bird	13 Mar. 51
22273754	Private D. Chalmers	13 Mar. 51
22158885	Private W. Gatt	13 Mar. 51
22272319	Private G. McKinnon	13 Mar. 51
22274534	Private J. Storer	13 Mar. 51
22117310	Private W. Taylor	3 April 51
14465416	Private D. Livie	4 April 51
14191015	Private D. Gilks	4 April 51
22248242	Private L. Young	4 April 51
19037310	Private M. Lee	4 April 51
412423	2nd Lieutenant A. C. Gilmour	6 April 51
22203304	Corporal H. Saunders	6 April 51
22203392	Private R. McNae	6 April 51
14466356	Private G. Morgan	6 April 51

14184719	Private J. Mulligan	6 April 51
22176735	Private A. Watson	6 April 51
21182500	Lance-Corporal D. Smith	6 April 51

MISSING

HILL 282

| 22274867 | Private B. Boatman | 23 Sept. 50 |
| 14189817 | Lance-Corporal J. Fielding | 23 Sept. 50 |

APPENDIX B

Decorations awarded during the Campaign *
(in the order of their publication)

Major K. Muir	Victoria Cross
	Silver Star (posthumous)
2nd Lieutenant M. D. W. Buchanan	Silver Star (posthumous)
Private W. Watts	Bronze Star Medal
Sergeant J. O'Sullivan M.M.	Bronze Star Medal
Lance-Corporal H. Ward	Bronze Star Medal
Sergeant E. Pigg	Bronze Star Medal (posthumous)
Lance-Corporal J. Fairhurst	Bronze Star Medal
Private E. Hill	Silver Star (posthumous)
Corporal R. Sweeney	Military Medal
Company Sergeant-Major T. Collett	Military Medal
Lieutenant-Colonel G. L. Neilson	Distinguished Service Order
	Silver Star
Captain C. N. A. Buchanan	Silver Star
Sergeant J. Robertson	Bronze Star Medal
Major J. B. Gillies	Silver Star
Corporal J. Walker	Bronze Star Medal
Major J. A. Penman M.C.	Bar to Military Cross
Major J. D. Stewart ⎱ M.B.E., M.C., T.D. ⎰	Officer, Order of the British Empire
	Bronze Star
Major J. B. M. Sloane	Officer, Order of the British Empire
Captain (Q.M.) A. W. Brown	Member, Order of the British Empire

Mentioned in Dispatches

Captain N. D. L Crowe
2nd Lieutenant J. R. R. Edington
Sergeant R. Smith
Lance-Corporal A. Mitchell
Private J. Smith
Private F. Satchwell
Private W. Farquharson
Private R. Wright
Captain A. J. Cookson

* The Silver Star and the Bronze Star Medal are American awards

PRINTED IN GREAT BRITAIN AT
THE PRESS OF THE PUBLISHERS